Leyton Orient: A Season in the Sun
1962-63

DESERT ISLAND FOOTBALL HISTORIES

Leyton Orient
A Season in the Sun
1962-63

Series Editor: Clive Leatherdale
Series Consultant: Leigh Edwards

Kevin Palmer

DESERT ISLAND BOOKS

First published in 2006
by
DESERT ISLAND BOOKS LIMITED
7 Clarence Road, Southend-on-Sea, Essex SS1 1AN
United Kingdom
www.desertislandbooks.com

British Library Cataloguing-in-Publication Data
A catalogue record for this book is available from the British Library

ISBN(10) 1-905328-05-2
IBSN(13) 978-905328-05-5

Printed in Great Britain
by
Biddles Ltd, King's Lynn

Photo credits: Vestry House Museum, London Borough of Waltham Forest;
David Block; Gordon Bolland; *Stratford Express*

Contents

Author's Note

This was a wonderful book to write. I'm sure that many Leyton Orient fans are unaware of the marvellous exploits of their side in reaching the old First Division – the pinnacle of English football. This isn't their fault. They are too young to have remembered it first hand and instead will have their own highlights, such as the run to the FA Cup semi-finals in 1977-78 or even the promotion out of the League's basement in 2005-06.

Football fans in general would barely notice Orient at the best of times, but there was this golden period from 1961 to 1963 when the club made themselves known throughout the land.

Many people have helped me along the way in writing this book. Several of the players who participated in these wonderful games have been invaluable in putting their own personal slant on proceedings, most notably Sid Bishop, Gordon Bolland, Stan Charlton, Dave Dunmore, Mal Lucas and Mike Pinner.

A special 'thank you' must go to a couple of the supporters who were present for many of these matches. Not only have Bryan Herman and David Block regaled me with memories of those distant days, but they have worked diligently to provide me with missing match reports, lists of referees, memorabilia from the time, and so forth. Without their assistance I would have had to work twice as hard as I did.

Jeff Powell of the *Daily Mail* (and once of the *Walthamstow Guardian*) was helpful, as were Matt Porter and Dave Dodd from Leyton Orient. Mark Wylie of the Manchester United museum helped me track down Johnny Carey's son.

I'm putting forward Leigh Edwards' name for a knighthood for services to footballing authors. This guy is a footballing encyclopaedia in human form, with an unerring ability to track down obscure facts and to find footballers who everyone else has forgotten about.

The Vestry House Museum in the London Borough of Waltham Forest also receives a special mention for holding the archives of the local newspapers and supplying most of the photographs reproduced in this book. Their staff are dedicated professionals who made my efforts so much easier. Also, thanks to all the local newspapers, most notably the *Walthamstow Guardian*, whose wonderful coverage of Leyton Orient over the years was so useful. The national newspapers also helped fill in the odd gaps. Thanks also to Gordon Bolland, who supplied some of his personal photographs for this book.

Lastly, I must thank my publisher Clive Leatherdale at Desert Island Books for commissioning me to write this, and if I've forgotten anybody who has helped me on my way, then I apologise profusely.

KEVIN PALMER
October 2006

Preface

I will never forget my first time at an Orient Supporters Club Dance. It was at a local pub called the Three Blackbirds, and because I was still in the Services this apprehensive young amateur player turned up in his Army uniform.

The fans immediately made me feel welcome and this happy atmosphere was present throughout my time with the club, from the chairman 'Happy' Harry Zussman all the way down. Though I left the club for three years to play for Arsenal, there was no hesitation when I had the chance to return to the Orient.

Johnny Carey took us up into the First Division with the minimum of effort, with his cries of 'Keep pushing it about lads!' as he puffed on his unlit pipe. Carey was not a tea-cup thrower in the dressing room at half-time. I was made captain some years before this, replacing the great Ken Facey, and I was very, very proud of this honour.

I was always very nervous about running out onto the pitch in case I tripped over, and the nerves only went when I got my first kick or tackle in. Being captain was a great responsibility and I recall asking Carey for a pay rise for the lads. Many managers would have just said that there was no money and walked away, but Carey took the trouble to show me the books to illustrate graphically why there was no money. Even though I had to tell the other players the bad news, I was chuffed to have been treated in such a way by the boss.

The game against Bury when we won promotion is always the one the fans remember, but to me it was just a blur with everything happening at once. I recall being chaired off the ground and surveying the wondrous scenes from the directors box, but it wasn't until I saw next season's programme with a front cover photo of that day that I could take it all in.

Our first game in the First Division was against my old club Arsenal, and it just happened to be my 100th game in the top flight. To be standing in the middle of the pitch, tossing a coin at the start of such a momentous match, was a dream.

Although we couldn't maintain our status with the top clubs, I was always extremely proud to play for the Orient. I always keep an eye out for their results and I love to come back for the reunion dinners. I'm honoured to be featured so prominently in this celebration of Orient's finest hour.

STAN CHARLTON

A Joke No Longer

(28 April 1962)

A Leyton Orient fan visits a fortune teller at the start of the 1961-62 season and asks her how Orient's season is going to go. She looks into her crystal ball and tells him that, going into the final game, Orient need a victory at home to Bury, and that their Second Division status rests on the outcome. The O's fan nods as she tells him this, as his team have only just performed a minor miracle to avoid relegation in the season just ended.

He asks her how the final match will end, but she says her crystal ball clouds over at that point. The fan is a great believer in League form, and he asks her how the games before that have gone.

She informs him that Orient will go into that final game not having won in the previous seven League matches at Brisbane Road. He thanks her, pays his money and walks away, and being a great believer in the powers of the fortune teller, resigns himself to yet another season of disappointment and heartache.

The excitement of the football season makes our supporter forget all about the words of the mystic lady after a few games, and it's only when he is standing on the terraces, watching his side running out on to the pitch for that fateful encounter with Bury, that he recalls her wise words.

Yes, his side have gone seven League games without a win at Brisbane Road, and yes, their Second Division status will rest on the outcome, only he naturally assumed that relegation was the likely outcome. Instead, to his continuing disbelief, his beloved side now stand on the verge of promotion to the First Division – that faraway land which he had always believed was out of reach of Leyton Orient – the running joke of London football.

He glances down at the new transistor radio in his hands, the one that cost him a large chunk of his weekly wage, and shakes his head gloomily. Not only does he have to watch his team and suffer the usual bout of agonies that they inflict upon him every week, but he now has to simultaneously listen in to the live second-half commentary from Swansea and double his anxiety by having to pray for the right result there too.

He shakes his head once more. In order to win promotion, Orient have to get a better result against Bury than Sunderland can achieve at Swansea, because both sides are level on points. Surely, there is no chance that Sunderland – the Bank of England team, who can seemingly go out and buy any player they want – could possibly fail to beat the lowly Welsh side.

To add to his woes, he knows that Sunderland have a slightly better goal-average, and that if both sides snatch an equal number of points on the day, it's going to take a quirky pair of results to turn things Orient's way.

To separate teams level on points, the League used to add up the goals scored by each club and divide that number by the total goals conceded, the higher the outcome the better. Our nervous fan had spent much of the day working out that if both sides were to draw their games, for example, Orient would only achieve promotion by making it a goalless draw, whilst requiring Sunderland to achieve an improbable 3-3 draw at least.

On the day, Orient took the lead on fourteen minutes. The ace goal-getter Dave Dunmore had whipped in a cross and Derek Gibbs had flicked it into the path of Mal Graham, whose back-header soared over Bury keeper Chris Harker.

Our man's wild whoop at that goal turned into a groan when he heard that Sunderland had also gone into the half-time interval with a 1-0 lead. Another scream of joy erupted round the ground when the radio commentator described a Swansea equaliser, then an explosion of ecstasy as, six minutes before the end, Mal Graham robbed a Bury player and tore into the heart of their box before unleashing a powerful shot into the back of the net.

Soon afterwards, the final whistle blew at both grounds and Orient's 2-0 victory and Sunderland's 1-1 draw was enough to send the London side into the top flight for the first (and so far the only time) in their history.

Whilst our delirious fan was busy chairing Mal Graham off the pitch, one Bury player knew that his poor marking for the first goal and fatal hesitation for the second had cost Sunderland promotion. He had stated earlier that Orient weren't as worthy of promotion as the mighty Rokerites.

Did he quietly resolve that day to make up for it somehow? Maybe, because that player was Bob Stokoe, who was destined to manage Sunderland to victory in the 1973 FA Cup final.

CHAPTER ONE

A Gentle Build-Up

Orient had been founded in 1888 as an offshoot of Glyn Cricket Club, not adopting the name of Orient until 1888, thanks to some of their players who worked for the Orient Shipping Line. They became known as Clapton Orient in 1898 and were by now playing at Whittles Athletic Ground. They moved to Millfields Road in 1900, and in 1905 joined the Second Division of the Football League. They twice finished fourth and remained in that division until being relegated to Division Three (South) in 1928-29. The following year they moved to Lea Bridge Road, but switched to their current home of Brisbane Road in 1937, changing their name to Leyton Orient immediately after the Second World War.

Leyton Orient had been perennial fixtures at the bottom of Division Three (South) when the first of the players who would eventually transform the fortunes of the club arrived. Sid Bishop had been the club mascot at Tooting & Mitcham, but soon after the War joined Chase of Chertsey, which was then Arsenal's nursery club. Sid recalls going away on tour with Chertsey and returning to find that they were now the nursery club of Leyton Orient. Alec Stock was by now manager of the O's, and the brilliant young boss soon gained a reputation for unearthing golden young talent at the most humble of surroundings. Young Sid began his Orient career in the unglamorous world of the groundstaff, but signed professional terms soon afterwards in May 1952, aged eighteen.

Bishop put on enough weight and height to progress from the youths to the reserves and in February 1954 made his debut in the first team as a centre-half. It took three years before he could make that No 5 shirt his own, and by then he was regarded as a very strong header of that fearsome leather ball, helped by a long neck which seemed to aid the amount of power he could generate when he connected with it. He was also an accomplished tackler, but his ball-playing skills were often overlooked. He made countless intelligent passes out of defence at a time when centre-backs tended to prefer the almighty hoofed clearance.

Given that Orient's later success was founded on the principles of short passing, this made his presence all the more necessary. He very rarely ventured beyond the halfway line though, and as a consequence averaged a goal only every 75 League games.

Stan Charlton joined Orient in the summer of 1952. Stan's dad had been good enough to turn out for an England representative side that went to Australia in 1925 and by the time Stan was born in June 1929 his dad was at Exeter City. Within a fortnight, dad had signed for Crystal Palace and Stan spent most of the war years in London, dodging the doodlebugs and playing football, because there was very little school. He tried to emulate his dad by joining Palace, but wasn't quite good enough. He was forced into National Service and played for various Army sides which helped him get a berth with Bromley FC. He played in the FA Amateur Cup final of 1952 and also played at Wembley against Scotland in an amateur international. This led to a call-up to the Olympic Squad at Helsinki that same year.

A friend had moved to Orient and told manager Alec Stock about the useful young right-back. Stock signed him that summer and immediately stuck him in the first team. He became a permanent fixture in the first team after that, his attacking instincts making him one of the very first of what we now call overlapping full-backs. This even led to a few games up front, but it was always as a full-back that this craggy-faced player excelled.

A move to Tottenham fell through because of a financial dispute between the two clubs, but Arsenal snapped him up for £30,000 in November 1955. He became a stalwart of that Gunners side, but fell out with manager George Swindin when he was appointed boss in 1958. Alec Stock wisely invested Orient club funds to bring him back and he soon permanently stitched himself into the No 2 jersey – or so it seemed.

Phil White was signed from Wealdstone in July 1953 at the age of 22. He was a scintillatingly quick player, but struggled initially because of a certain shyness that prevented him from showing his best qualities. The elfin-like player with the hooded eyes and large ears finally overcame that timidity and welded himself into the outside-right position, partly because he was a one-footed player, only using his left peg in emergencies. He had the chance to join Liverpool in 1956 but turned down the £15,000 move, preferring to stay in his familiar surroundings.

Not only was Alec Stock an astute buyer of cheap talent, but he blended the side together well too. The manager, who had first come to prominence as the man who had guided non-league Yeovil's FA Cup victory over First Division Sunderland in 1949, proved that that was no fluke as he transformed Orient's prospects. By 1953-54 they made it into the top half of the Third Division (South) and then the following season finished runners-up to runaway champions Bristol City. In those days only the champions were promoted, but the disappointment was soon forgotten as Orient strode to the title the following season, with Bishop, Charlton and White all aiding the cause. They broke several club records on the way. Their points total of 66 and goals total of 106 were exceptional, both of which were enhanced by an 8-0 demolition of Crystal Palace in November 1955 and a 7-1 win over QPR in March 1956. By the time of that win over Rangers, Alec Stock had left to join Arsenal, leaving trainer Les Gore in charge, but Stock only stayed at Highbury for 53 days before rushing back to Orient once more. It was where his heart was.

Gore proved his merit by signing star striker Tommy Johnston from Newport and the prolific marksman played a major role in keeping Orient in the Second Division. Also useful was Frank George, who was busy keeping goals out at the other end from 1957 onwards. He had been signed from Carshalton Athletic in July 1954 as a teenager, but the young keeper had to wait patiently for three years to displace Pat Welton and Dave Groombridge from between the posts. George was a whisker under 6ft tall, but was very muscular and strong. He didn't have particularly quick reactions, but was often spotted dashing off his line to pluck a teasing cross out of the air. He found it hard to maintain his form though, and only in 1958-59 did he make over 30 League appearances in a single season.

Orient kept themselves safely away from trouble in their first season back in Division Two, but Stock knew his team needed strengthening if it was to do better. He signed Ron Foster from Clapton in March 1957 and the inside-forward became a fixture in the youths and reserves over the next few years, finally making his debut for the first team in October 1959.

Making a quicker impression on the side was Cyril Lea, who was signed from Bradley Rangers in his native Wales in July 1957. He began his career as a left-back and was playing in that position by the time he made Orient's first team in February 1958. After a year he was converted into a left-half. Although he was not a tall player, he was quite strong and stocky and delighted in dispossessing opponents. He loved to have the ball and was forever calling for it, his Welsh tones being a familiar sound at Brisbane Road over the years as he let everyone know he was around.

Orient made it up to halfway in Division Two in 1957-58 and the squad was improved further by capturing another teenager – namely Joe Elwood from Glenavon. The Belfast boy was capped at Schoolboy, Under-23 and 'B' international level with Northern Ireland and preferred to play as an inside-left. His sheer versatility made him an expert in providing cover for other positions though, and he became used chiefly as a utility player, filling in for injured men and using his versatility to great effect. This jack-of-all-trades ability meant he is often overlooked when the promotion side of 1961-62 is recalled.

George Wright was already a long-established right-back with West Ham when Orient picked him up in May 1958. The 28-year-old began his career with three Kent clubs – Ramsgate, Thanet and Margate – before making the breakthrough with the Hammers. Wright was getting on a bit by the time the promotion team hit its peak and he very rarely took the place of Stan Charlton.

Eddie Lewis joined at around the same time as Wright and was another player who spent a lot of time fighting for his first-team place, this time as a left-back. He had been one of the original Busby Babes, playing twenty times in the League and scoring an impressive nine goals between 1952 and 1955. He joined Preston in December 1955, but stayed less than a year before coming down to West Ham. He did well at the Hammers, adding a dozen goals in a year and a half before Orient signed him. Lewis was an unusual sight in the No 3 shirt, because he was much bigger than the archetypal left-back, frightening many a delicate right-winger with his sheer physical bulk. This made him somewhat slow by full-back standards, but he was intelligent enough to overcome this handicap.

Not only was Cyril Lea quite vocal on the pitch, he wasn't shy in suggesting to Alec Stock that a teammate of his at Bradley Rangers would be worth signing. Mal Lucas had been a player with Wrexham, Bolton and Liverpool, but failed to make any impression with any of them, not helped by never being quite sure of what position he was supposed to be. He had spells as a forward and as a midfielder, but finally settled down as a right-half with Orient, taking the place of the ageing Ken Facey. Although not regarded as being quite as skilful as Lea, he was the better tackler and the two players complemented each other perfectly. He was still an excellent player overall and this was reflected in his winning of Welsh international honours whilst at Orient.

George Waites was signed from Harwich & Parkestone in December 1958, even though he was a Stepney boy. He was primarily a right-winger but often found it difficult to win a first-team place from players like Phil White. Terry McDonald was also a Stepney lad, but he played on the opposite wing. He was on West Ham's books but never got a game in the first team before Orient persuaded him to join them. The tiny little blond winger scored on his debut in October 1959, but really came to prominence by destroying Middlesbrough in the next home game. McDonald was very fast, and used his tiny frame to excellent effect by body-swerving his way round opponents. He was an excellent crosser of the ball and also loved to have a pot-shot at goal, but like many of his colleagues up front, he was prone to 'disappear' during games when his form took a dip.

Orient frequently used to nip over the Scottish border to check up on the local footballing talent and Bill Taylor was signed at the start of the 1959-60 season from the delightfully named outfit of Bonnyrigg Rose. He was predominately a left-back, though Eddie Lewis's proficiency in that department meant he had to be versatile enough to play in positions such as outside-right. He had only just reached the age of twenty when Orient signed him and they never really saw him at his best as he was a late developer.

Orient began to struggle a bit at the start of the 1960s, but still the team was made stronger for the future. Mal Graham was 26 years old when Orient signed him from Bristol City, but he had made most of his reputation at Barnsley where he had played over a hundred games as an inside-forward, scoring 35 League goals. The Tykes had got him from the minnows of Hall Green, but by the time he reached Orient he was a seasoned professional. He was once described as a 'bustling opponent who caused a great deal of trouble to opposing defences with his opportunism', which may sound like a euphemism for a dirty player, but that is too cruel a suggestion. He was physical, but used his strength intelligently to steal past defenders and unleash powerful shots which so often resulted in a bulging net.

Bill Robertson was a keeper in a similar mould to Frank George, being quiet and steady rather than quick and showy, but he was generally a reliable custodian. He was a Glaswegian, born way back in 1928 and he had begun his career with Arthurlie. He was snapped up by Chelsea in time for the resumption of post-War League football in 1946 and made 199 League appearances for them over the next fourteen years. Confusingly, Chelsea had two goalkeepers on their books between 1946 and 1948 with the name Bill Robertson, and the other one went on to play for Birmingham and Stoke. Our Bill was a big, broad-shouldered individual and in the promotion game against Bury made a couple of saves that perhaps neither George or Pinner would have reached with their smaller frames.

Derek Gibbs was also acquired from Chelsea, but the inside-forward had only played 23 League games in five years. He struggled to maintain a permanent place in Orient's side, too, after signing in November 1960 and had to content himself with various roles such as left-half and inside-left as well as his more favoured position of inside-right.

Orient's Division Two status was in severe danger of ending by the time Ron Newman joined in January 1961 from Portsmouth. The left-winger (originally from Woking) helped stabilise things on the left-wing, but it was the inspired signature of Dave Dunmore in March 1961 that really saved their bacon. The strapping striker had played for York Boys and Cliftonville Minors before making his name at York City from 1952 onwards. Spurs made an exciting £10,500 bid for him in February 1954 and he played for six years, leaving just before the great double side did its business in 1960-61. Instead he had to watch that team from the comparative backwaters of West Ham, though it must have seemed like another step down when he was offered the Orient striking job in March 1961. Going the other way in that deal was Alan Sealey, who was to score both Hammers goals in the European Cup-Winners' Cup final in May 1965. Dunmore helped Orient win two of their last four games and they avoided relegation by just three points. Nobody could have predicted the destiny of Orient by the end of the following season.

CHAPTER TWO

Same Again Johnny

(August-October 1961)

Leyton Orient's 1961-62 season began with a change of manager. Les Gore had always been a reluctant boss and with a sigh of relief he handed over his managerial suit and donned his trainer's clobber once more. The board were well aware that the club were merely treading water in the Second Division and were in grave danger of a return back to the small pond that was Division Three. The board had been wise in sticking with Gore, waiting until the right man came along, but with the ex-Everton manager Johnny Carey available, the club tempted him along to Brisbane Road.

Johnny Carey was only 42 when he was appointed Orient boss in August 1961, but with his balding pate and quiet air of authority that came with an enormous reputation, he looked ten years older. He was born in Dublin and was playing for a local side called St James' Gate when Manchester United paid the handsome sum of £250 to acquire his services in November 1936. He had just started to establish himself in the United side, initially as an inside-left, when the Second World War broke out. Though the Irish Republic declared itself neutral, Carey saw it as his duty to defend his adopted country, and he saw action in the Middle East and Italy.

Carey returned to Old Trafford after the War, and thrived under the stewardship of their new manager Matt Busby. Although most fans are aware of the legendary Busby Babes, who were nearly wiped out in the slush at Munich Airport in 1958, and the 1968 side that captured the European Cup, it is often overlooked that Busby had built up an equally great side in the late 1940s and early 50s. Busby was astute enough to recognise the ability that resided inside Carey and he was soon appointed captain.

By this time, Carey was established as a full-back, but he was sufficiently versatile and intelligent to be able to adapt himself to various roles, and the only positions that he never played in for United were goalkeeper and outside-right. Manchester United had been a mediocre club in English football since the First World War, but with Busby's inspired management and Carey's equally assured leadership on the pitch, the Red Devils became a major force at the top of the table. Carey held aloft the FA Cup in 1948, but it seemed as though he was never going to get his hands on a League Championship trophy, because in four years out of five between 1946-47 and 1950-51 they finished runners-up to Liverpool, Arsenal, Portsmouth and Tottenham respectively. Finally in 1951-52 they won the title, but by then Busby was aware that his side had peaked and it was time to bring on the youths. Carey hung on another year before retiring, and although Busby offered him a coaching role, he turned it down in favour of a move into management.

Blackburn Rovers were the club that took on the services of the 1949 Footballer of the Year, and winner of 29 'southern' Ireland and seven Northern Ireland caps – one of 34 players to have been capped by the two Irelands up to 1951. In his five seasons at Ewood Park from 1953, he took them from Second Division mediocrity and eventually into the First Division in 1958, when they also reached the FA Cup semi-finals.

By 1958 Everton were also a club that traded on past glories and they hadn't won a trophy since the Second World War and had even suffered the ignominy of a three-season spell in the Second Division. The Toffees appointed Carey as the boss to right these wrongs, and although they didn't do very well in his first two seasons, once they were bankrolled by the Littlewoods Pools magnate John Moores, Carey lifted them up to fifth in 1960-61, their highest position for 22 years. Unfortunately, with Moores as the new chairman, success wasn't happening quickly enough for the impatient board and Carey was relieved of his duties in April 1961. The dirty deed of sacking him was carried out in the inappropriate place of the back of a London taxi after a Football League meeting.

And so, Orient chairman Harry Zussman was at his charming best to persuade Carey that a move to the Second Division strugglers was a good career move. Though Carey was going back to a similar situation he inherited when he joined Blackburn in 1953, he went about his task with the same degree of professionalism and fortitude that he had always displayed.

Carey cast an eye round the set-up at Brisbane Road and saw that with the combination of Eddie Baily as assistant manager and Les Gore as trainer, he didn't need to make wholesale changes amongst the back-room boys, which was reassuring to the players, who craved continuity rather than revolution. It's unlikely that Carey was entirely happy with the contents of his playing squad, but there was no money given to him to change the side, so he had to make do with what he had acquired for the time being.

Carey's first chance to assess his new charges under playing conditions came in the traditional curtain-raiser to the new season – The Blues versus The Reds – in other words, the first team against the reserves. Some teams dubbed this 'The Probables' versus 'The Possibles', but most teams opted to differentiate them by the colours of the playing strip, namely the first and second choice.

Orient have found it difficult to settle on a name for themselves over the years and have had equal difficulties deciding what to wear on the pitch. In 1961 it was the reserves that sported red, whilst the first team favoured blue shirts with white edging, white shorts, and white stockings with blue trim. The blue was a shade somewhere in between the sky blue later adopted by Coventry and the royal blue of Everton. The numbers of the players were picked out in a large, white, iron-on digits.

Carey, Baily and Gore worked between them to choose their favoured eleven for the Blues, and given that the eleven they chose for this match was exactly the same line-up that was to become so familiar in the first part of the season, they were shrewd and decisive in their choices. Bill Robertson retained his place in goal. Stan Charlton stayed in his favoured right-back role, having spent much of the previous season as left-back. Eddie Lewis managed to nail down the left-back's role, whilst Mal Lucas wore the right-half's No 4 shirt. Veteran Sid Bishop was an automatic choice at centre-half and there were no surprises either at the appearance of Cyril Lea at left-half. Phil White kept his place on the right wing, having done well in the O's side that had lifted themselves clear of the drop at the end of last season, and Terry McDonald was favoured on the opposite flank. Ron Foster and Mal Graham had spent all of last season competing for the inside-left shirt, but both were accommodated by switching Foster to the inside-right's berth.

Someone had to make way for Foster, and this provided the biggest eye-opener. Tommy Johnston was a legend at Brisbane Road, and the rugged Scotsman's total of 35 League goals in a season (1957-58) and 121 in total has never been bettered by an Orient player to this day. The barnstorming centre-forward, so lethal in the air, had played a major part in getting Orient into the Second Division and keeping them there, but he was just about to turn 34 and was deemed too old by Carey for the coming campaign. Instead he had to take his place amongst the reserves for this fixture – which must have been a bitter pill to swallow for one so rightly proud of his achievements.

Other players in the Reds' reserve team were keeper Albert Cochran, who had played in the final League game of the previous season, which Carey had used as an experiment to find his ideal line-up. Poor Cochran was destined never to turn out for the first team again. Two previous stalwarts of the side who didn't play in the first team in the next two seasons were Dennis Sorrell, who found it impossible the break open the Lucas-Bishop-Lea half-back line (though he returned in the mid-1960s), and Ken Facey, an inside-forward with an impressive total of 74 League goals for Orient, but who was of a similar vintage to Johnston and was also put out to grass in the reserves. George Wright, Ron Newman, Bill Taylor, Derek Gibbs and Joe Elwood had a more realistic chance of earning a place in the elite and we shall hear these names again later.

The Friday-night game itself was a total mismatch and the Reds ran out easy 6-0 winners. White grabbed a couple of goals, with the others being shared out between Graham, Lewis, Lea and Dunmore, but surprisingly the attack was much criticised in the press as being ineffectual. The service up to the lone centre-forward Dunmore was patchy against very poor-looking opposition and this meant that Dunmore was isolated for much of the game, though he did test Cochran at frequent intervals, only beating the rookie keeper with a 30-yarder near the end. The preferred defence was solid against the weak Reds attack, but there was little to suggest that this season was going to be anything more than a repeat of the previous season's struggles. Indeed, manager Carey publicly declared: 'there will be no wild claims for the First Division this season. Our first job is to consolidate Orient's position in Division Two. I want football – the pure stuff. Play it, and the goals will come.'

Carey certainly had headaches to contend with on the eve of the new season, because Foster, Graham, Lucas and Sorrell had all rejected the one-season contracts that had been offered by the club. Their grievances boiled down to a combination of wanting the security of a longer contract and the lack of money on offer. Up till the previous season, a maximum wage of £20 a week was in existence, and though most Orient players weren't employed on wages that high, they were at least not far behind even the best players in the country.

With that barrier removed, players like Fulham's Johnny Haynes were getting as much as £100 a week, and the gap between the rich and poor clubs was suddenly a yawning chasm. Cash-strapped Orient were in no position to spend more money on the wage bill, so they dug their heels in. The players pleaded with the FA to mediate for them, but in the end it was common sense that prevailed. The players had nowhere else to go and the club had no money to replace them, so a compromise was found. At other clubs there would have been an undercurrent of unhappiness seeping through the squad, but the geniality of 'Gentleman John' Carey (his nickname at Old Trafford) was enough to ensure that everyone was persuaded to stay happy and pulling in the same direction.

Carey was handed the toughest of tests for his new side when they had to travel up to play Newcastle United in the opening fixture. The Magpies were back down in the Second Division for the first time in thirteen years, and nobody was quite sure whether they would bounce straight back up or not.

Carey wasn't fazed by the occasion and the players were reassured by his quiet, positive manner that banished any negative thoughts from their mind. They were now getting used to the sight of the unlit brown pipe that seemed to be a permanent fixture in Carey's mouth. There were very few instructions; he just let players get on with playing the way they knew how.

Newcastle United fans have a reputation for getting behind their team, no matter how poorly their side are doing, but the crowd of 26,638 couldn't even fill half of St James' Park. The lack of atmosphere seemed to percolate through to their players, because there was a distinct lack of passion from the home side. The two international-class inside-forwards, Ivor Allchurch (Wales) and Liam Tuohy (Ireland) were trying harder than anyone wearing stripes, but they were easily contained by Lucas and Charlton. Orient were causing problems on the left wing for United all the game, with left-back Lewis rushing forward on overlapping runs, despite his lack of pace due to his big build. McDonald streaked to and fro, terrorising Dick Keith at right-back one minute and then sprinting back to cover for Lewis's runs the next. Despite this effort, there was still not much goalmouth action for the handful of visiting O's fans to enjoy and it wasn't until late on that McDonald nearly snatched a deserved win.

The general opinion from pundits and fans was that Orient should be OK for that mid-table position on this showing, with the sound defence precluding relegation and the weak attack foiling a promotion bid.

Most O's fans had neither the disposable income nor the time to go and see their team in action away from Leyton, so the first home game of the season was eagerly awaited by many. Southampton were a good match for the O's, with a granite outcrop at the heart of their defence in the form of the gigantic Tony Knapp and a lively forward line that tested the home side's offside tactics to the full. After an hour it was honours even at 1-1 (Foster having headed in from a corner for Orient), but the Saints were just that bit more clinical in front of goal. Terry Paine was already an experienced winger (into his fifth of a total of eighteen seasons with the club) and his cross to Tom Mulgrew was headed in to make it 1-2. Mulgrew added a second soon afterwards and Orient were sunk.

It would have been a heavier defeat had Lea not rugby-tackled George O'Brien as the Saint bore down ominously on goal. The sinner escaped with a mere booking – nothing less than attempted murder would get you sent off in those days – but the crowd hated such blatantly unsporting behaviour and even the home fans booed their errant player. It must be emphasised that football was not played in a bubble where Corinthian values reigned though – it was usually hard; it was often dirty.

On paper, the 2-0 home win over Middlesbrough was a comfortable one, but football is played on grass and there was much criticism of Orient's attacking prowess. Thankfully for the nerves of the fans, Orient scored early on. A McDonald cross evaded Dunmore, but racing in behind him was Phil White who steered the ball in.

Players like McDonald knew where White would be, welded into his outside-right position, because he was one-footed. White was very fast, but Stan Charlton was quicker still and was once placed third in a race between the fastest footballing sprinters in London. Even Stan acknowledges that reserve keeper Dave Groombridge had the edge on him though. This was often evident on Friday nights, when sprint training was enlivened by the placing of bets on the outcome.

There was no whingeing about Orient's strong half-back line of Lucas, Bishop and Lea, and there was much relief that Lucas had signed a new contract and was now happy. Graham was still not satisfied with his proposed terms and he was still holding out.

A couple of northern sides were rumoured to have made offers that were not good enough for the club and it was generally felt amongst the fans that such a clever link-man should be re-signed quickly. Another unhappy player was reserve full-back George Wright. Carey had suggested training in the afternoons, which interfered with Wright's second job as a carpenter. Eventually a compromise was found and Wright stayed.

Traditionally the second and fourth League matches of the season were played against the same opposition, so Orient made the trip along the south coast to play Southampton again. There was little for anyone to cheer in the first half and the match only came to life after Terry O'Brien gave the Saints the lead early in the second half. A repeat of the defeat of nine days previously seemed likely, but Graham was inspirational in preventing the Saints from marching on, and Foster's snap shot and McDonald's long-range howitzer ensured away-day joy.

Graham and Foster finally signed new contracts in time for another day trip on the train, this time for Walsall. With any lingering doubts about their future quashed, the two players performed with a *joie de vivre* that permeated through the whole team.

Carey and Baily had been drumming their ideas into the team persistently, and now everything they wanted came to fruition. Carey's easy-going approach to management fostered a strong spirit of camaraderie and cooperation. Baily was tougher and he worked hard at the practicalities of playing as a single unit on the pitch. Lucas remembers playing in a match against Spurs Reserves a few years before and getting annihilated by a rampant Baily. The Spurs legend encouraged the disheartened Welshman by telling him that the game was all about learning. Orient were learning fast.

There was very little wrong at the back anyway, but now the inside-forwards and wingers worked together with a purpose and the forwards responded by gelling in a way that the visiting handful of O's fans could barely remember. Orient were already cruising at 2-0 up, when Graham went crazy with a hat-trick in less than fifteen minutes midway through the second half.

Firstly he got on the end of Lewis's through ball, but looked to have taken it too far before deceiving keeper John Christie with a shot that squeezed past him at an unlikely angle. Dunmore set him up with an easy drive for his second and then he wrapped up the win with a sweetly hit effort from the edge of the area. Poor Walsall hadn't been beaten at Fellows Park for seventeen months, but they were merely also-rans as Orient racked up their best away win since they thrashed Torquay United 7-2 in 1954.

Most teams can manage an impressive win now and again, but the real test comes in the following game. Is it a fluke, or are things really coming together? Derby were the team who were being experimented on at Brisbane Road, but there was still a general feeling of apathy amongst the casual fans.

Orient's accountants reckoned that gates of 15,000 were required in order for the team to make money, but only 12,316 fans clicked through the turnstiles today.

Quite why Orient could only survive on such high gates is something of a mystery. The overheads must have been quite low. Very little had been spent on the ground (though to be fair, very little was spent on any ground in those days); the wages bill was still low despite the abolition of the maximum wage, and the board weren't hoarding cash for a splurge on new players either. It's true that Orient had to share their home gate receipts with the opposition club then, but they also got half of the away revenue in return. The only noticeably higher cost to the club this season was the number of win bonuses being paid out, but Harry Zussman wasn't exceptionally generous in that department either.

Many fans from outside London would reckon it was easy for Orient's fans to get to the game, but you didn't have to live many miles from the ground for it to become a logistical nightmare. Bryan Herman, a keen Orienteer, lived about three miles away in Bow at the time. He used to hop on the bus to Bethnal Green Underground Station and then catch the train to Leyton. When funds were tight he used to walk across Hackney Marshes, but that wasn't something worth contemplating on a wet winter night. He later moved to Brentwood in Essex, which involved a train ride to Stratford and a Central Line tube to Leyton Underground Station. Buses were also available, but they were invariably packed as very few people owned cars.

The Orient players had no difficulty finding their way round the Brisbane Road pitch and the home fans enjoyed a cracking game as Derby attacked with verve, though their finishing never matched their intent. On another day they might have punished the O's, but they went into the break a goal behind when winger Ray Swallow tried to help out his defence and only succeeded in sliding Dunmore's pass beyond his bemused keeper.

The points were wrapped up from the penalty spot after Tony Conwell handled the ball after tackling McDonald. Obviously he didn't 'con well' enough.

The O's were now second in the table, but it was still far too early to make any judgments as to how the rest of the season would pan out.

	P	Pts
1 Liverpool	6	12
2 ORIENT	6	9
3 Huddersfield	6	9
4 Walsall	7	9
5 Bury	6	8
6 Rotherham	5	8
7 Scunthorpe	6	8

Orient took a long train journey up north for a Monday evening encounter with Fourth Division strugglers Stockport in the League Cup. The competition was in its second season and was regarded with about as much enthusiasm as the Anglo-Italian Cup or the Full Members' Cup would be in later years, yet all but the very top sides were prepared to give it a chance.

County gave their all, but didn't have the *nous* to beat Orient's famed defence that was regularly defying players of a much higher calibre. Even when George was beaten, Charlton was positioned on the line to clear. McDonald garnered the winner by following up on his own blocked long-range shot. Carey made his first change of the season in playing Joe Elwood instead of Foster, but reverted back to his favoured eleven for the next League match.

All good things must come to an end, but it was galling that the four-match unbeaten away run and the five-match winning streak came to an end against a Bristol Rovers side that had lost every League game so far. For once, the Leyton Orient defence was downright sloppy and goalkeeper George was criticised for his positioning for both of the Rovers goals. The attack reverted to lacklustre and it's telling that the late consolation came from the penalty spot after Ray Mabbutt (father of footballers Gary and Kevin) upended the eventual goalscorer, Dunmore.

Gratifyingly, Orient bounced back quickly with a superlative display at Brisbane Road, which left fancied Huddersfield well-beaten by half-time. Admittedly, a pulled muscle sustained by centre-half John Coddington ruined Town's chances as the poor man was forced to limp on as a winger and then a striker (this was four years before substitutes were allowed).

Even so, it was wonderful to see accomplished players like future England World Cup left-back Ray Wilson being turned inside-out by the marauding home side. Two goals midway through the first half settled things, and Graham made it 3-0 soon after the break. It was also pleasing to see that Carey didn't panic after the Rovers defeat and make changes to the line-up as most managers would have done. He was astute enough to realise that his side were generally sound, but not good enough to play well every week. He accepted that every now and again they would under-perform and lose, but that there was no need to panic.

There had been much panicking at Deepdale following Preston's relegation to the Second Division at the end of the previous season. They were still regarded as a top team, and just over three years ago had finished runners-up in the Championship. Now they were bumping along at the foot of the Second Division and the huge crowds that greeted the recently retired Tom Finney were a memory. Fewer than 10,000 were inside the cauldron of Deepdale for Orient's first visit since 1928, but somehow the home fans inspired their team into an unlikely three-goal lead with fifteen minutes remaining.

Like the last away game, the confidence of the weary, struggling side was lifted by an early goal, when an overhead cross by Dave Sneddon was enthusiastically volleyed in by Peter Thompson. Further goals came in early in the second half as Preston maintained the attacking momentum, but like many sides unused to being in such a position, they completely switched off near the end. This prompted Orient into a late two-goal rally and only a lack of time prevented a draw or a win, as Preston's hapless defence ran around like headless chickens, colliding with each other and scaring their fans witless.

There was also a spot of turmoil at Brisbane Road, with a couple of noticeable departures. Striker Tom Johnston had become a legend by cracking in 70 goals in a mere 87 League games before a short-lived move to Blackburn in 1958. He returned to Leyton the following year when he added another 51 goals in 93 League games. His aggregate of 121 League goals and his 35 goals in the 1957-58 season are both figures unmatched by any Orient player to date.

Johnston had just turned 34 and was no longer part of Carey's plans, though it was Carey who, as Blackburn Rovers manager, had signed Johnston in the first place. The out-of-favour marksman had helped to destroy Gillingham in last season's FA Cup and the Gills boss Harry Barratt was keen to add him to his lowly Fourth Division side's squad.

An earlier attempt had stalled, due to Johnston apparently being unhappy with his share of the deal, which upset Barratt: 'It is a great pity, for he possesses that which I need most of all in a player – the know-how. This does not come, in my opinion, until a player is around the 29 mark, and at 34 Johnston is a fine footballer in whom I shall continue to be interested.'

Barratt was true to his word and after some juggling with the fee in order to steer more money into Johnston's pocket he departed for about £3,000. He stayed there for a year, before becoming player-coach at Folkestone and finally becoming a bookie in Lancashire. He later emigrated to Australia, where he still lives.

The other departure was reserve-team trainer Nick Collins, who used to train the first team when Gore was manager. Now Gore had reverted back to first-team trainer and the club reckoned he could handle the reserves as well, thus reducing the wage bill by making Collins redundant.

Typically the first team would train seriously for about 90 minutes in the morning, five days a week at various locations around the area, including Snakes Lane in Woodford, Hackney Marshes, Epping Forest, and numerous places for roadwork. Afternoons were generally more relaxed, and the players tended to concentrate on their ball skills in the snooker hall. Phil White was the best player with the cue and frequently used to supplement his wages by winning money off the others. Dennis Sorrell was still at the club, but despite signing a new deal, was still asking for a move.

Anyone still under the misapprehension that football was a gentler game in the early 1960s, with impeccably-behaved crowds, should be transported back in time to Leeds Road, Huddersfield on Wednesday, 27 September 1961. The home fans were piqued when their defender Bob Parker was carried off with a dislocated shoulder following a spirited challenge from an unknown Orient player.

They were even more upset when White nipped in from the right wing to give the O's the lead, but were apoplectic when an excitable McDonald was booked by the referee in the second half as he over-reacted to some tough tackling meted out by unforgiving Yorkshiremen. The angry home support began to pelt poor visiting keeper George with any objects that came to hand, and he was forced to call on the help of the police in order to save him from injury. The home fans were placated to some extent by a late equaliser that was nevertheless undeserved.

This was followed by a rare Friday night game, which swelled the crowd figure to over 13,000 and it's a reasonably safe assumption that the extra souls weren't visiting Plymouth fans. Instead, many of the newcomers would have been supporters of other clubs, especially Arsenal who were playing away the next day. Orient were fondly (though somewhat patronisingly) regarded by fans of the Gunners, Spurs and Hammers, and there was a regular contingent of visitors from these clubs when their own team weren't playing at home.

Those neutrals would have expected more from Orient, but once more the team were dozing at the start of the game and succumbed to an early goal. The scorer was Keith Williams, who also added a second just before half-time. The harassed reporter from one local paper called him 'Frank' and his confusion is understandable.

In addition to Keith Williams (whose real first name was Ron), Argyle also had a pair of players called John Williams, though thankfully for the addled scribe they dropped one of them for this match. The last of the Johns to join Argyle was called 'Cardiff' Williams after the club they bought him from.

The reporter made up for this minor mistake by accurately underlining the common failing that was to bedevil Orient over the next couple of years – the lack of firepower up front. The midfield saw enough of the ball, but not enough chances were given to the underworked forward line in the first half. Orient's relied heavily on the passing game, unlike many of their cruder opponents, and the journalist was right to wonder if their game would completely go to pot on the muddier winter grounds, as they had done the previous season. Dunmore did see more of the ball in the second half, but he wasn't in a productive mood and only managed a consolation goal at the end. Orient were already relying too heavily on him and the lack of a younger version of Johnston to help him was mentioned.

The reserve-team players must have been perpetually chomping at the bit by this time, because nobody had been injured and Carey hadn't dropped anybody during these first eleven League games. The second string played midweek games in the Football Combination, but were given a bit of variety when half of them turned out in a game against Enfield in the London Challenge Cup. The rest of Orient's side were youths and third-teamers, but they did themselves no favours by being comfortably beaten 1-3 at Brisbane Road by the all-amateur Athenian League side. For the record it was Ron Newman who scored a late consolation goal following a dash from the right wing.

Joe Elwood did get another run out in the first team in place of Foster in the League Cup second round, and Carey's hand was forced into making one change as Dunmore had picked up a minor knock. Derek Gibbs was more of an inside-forward than a striker, which perhaps explains a lot of Orient's woes up front.

The opponents were Blackpool, who were still in the top flight, but who were definitely on the wane. They had finished in the top ten in all but one season in the 1950s but had only just escaped relegation the season before. The Seasiders were synonymous with Stanley Matthews, but the 46-year-old genius was a frustrated observer, being on the verge of a transfer to Stoke City at the time. Without their talisman, Blackpool looked little more than a mediocre Second Division side and Orient easily contained them, even late on when the Tangerines piled extra bodies forward in search of a winner. Orient had innumerable chances to kill the game off, but without even their one recognised striker they were toothless tigers.

Blackpool took the lead immediately after the restart, when the entire O's defence seemed to don clown's outfits as they failed to deal with a straightforward cross. Gibbs relieved some of the tension after an hour when his shot was helped into the net by goalkeeper Gordon West. The 10,000 crowd inside Brisbane Road were annoyed. They knew Orient should have won instead of earning a replay at the end of the month.

Dunmore returned to the side for the home League game against Stoke and this ensured that the same eleven players all featured in the opening twelve games – a quite astonishing achievement. Not only had the team collectively managed to avoid picking up injuries, which was some doing, given the tough tackling that came as standard in those days, but Carey had doggedly refused to make changes, even when individuals had suffered an off-day, and given the fact they were fourth in the table it was a wise move.

Footballers are a conservative bunch generally and they tend to operate at their most efficient when they are dealing with the familiar. Eddie Baily had worked hard with the side, getting them to operate the push and run system to a high standard. Given that the system requires an almost telepathic understanding of where one's colleagues are and where they will be running to, the fact that the players around them were always the same made life so much easier, and much of the slick passing was achieved without any conscious thought. Elwood may have been a decent replacement for Foster in the League Cup-ties, but his positioning and runs were naturally different and the players around him had to adjust to that, which made life a tad more difficult for them.

The benefits of a consistent line-up were amply demonstrated in the first half against Stoke, when the O's were rampant. Superb passing, clever running off the ball, and incisive finishing led to a 3-0 half-time lead without any apparent effort. Stoke looked like a set of players who had never met before. The home element inside the 10,000 crowd who were enjoying this feast of football were therefore miffed when Orient came out for the second half and merely went through the motions. If you asked the O's fans before the game how they would react if their team were 3-0 up and cruising, not many would have suggested a chorus of booing and slow hand-clapping, but that's exactly what they did. If Stoke hadn't been the most inept side to have played against them this season, then they may have been punished for their casualness, but they weren't.

Carey was finally forced to make a change for the thirteenth League match, when an injured Graham was replaced by Derek Gibbs. The lack of first-team action was immediately apparent as the nervous stand-in missed three good opportunities early on, in front of a huge 36,000 gate at Roker Park. Dunmore soon showed him how to shoot, but despite playing attractive football, they could not capitalise on their 1-0 lead.

The reason was, quite simply, down to one man – Brian Clough. The striker had just set a new record by racking up 200 League goals in just 219 games and he showed no inclination to ease up against the O's. He whipped in a couple of shots that poor Frank George couldn't cope with. Clough's first, midway through the first half, spun out of George's hands, rolled over his chest and trickled over the line. The hapless keeper couldn't get anywhere near Clough's winner early in the second half, though. The O's 1-2 defeat was ample proof that pretty play was no substitute for ruthless finishing and Orient didn't get any points for being regarded as the best team to have played at Roker Park that season.

Orient's excellent start to the campaign received official recognition when England manager Walter Winterbottom sent the ex-England captain Billy Wright down to Brisbane Road to cast his eye over inside-right Ronnie Foster for a possible inclusion into their Under-23 squad. Both Orient and Rotherham were surprise names near the top of the table, but nobody would have guessed it on this showing. Foster had a poor game, like almost everyone else who wasn't a defender. It took until early in the second half for the deadlock to be broken and that was a half-chance snapped up by a grateful Graham. The Merry Millers levelled from the spot after Bill Cassidy was adjudged to have been fouled by Lea, despite George getting a hand to Peter Perry's penalty. The poor O's fans suffered further when Ken Houghton dribbled round George in the last minute, but the gasp of relief was audible when he hit the post with his shot.

Orient lost the Essex Professional Cup final 1-2 to Colchester United, despite fielding a strong side, but this was a minor distraction as Saturday, 28 October saw the biggest game of the season for Orient so far – the visit to Anfield. A glance at the League table will reveal the significance.

	P	Pts
1 Liverpool	14	21
2 Southampton	15	18
3 Derby	14	17
4 Sunderland	14	16
5 Rotherham	13	16
6 ORIENT	14	15

It's hard to imagine now, but Liverpool were in their eighth consecutive season as a Second Division club, with a history of just being pipped at the post for promotion. Less than three years ago they had been humbled by non-league Worcester City in the FA Cup and they were a shambolic outfit. Bill Shankly had been appointed manager in November 1959, but a lack of cash had ruined his prospects for strengthening the team.

By the spring of 1961 the money had been found and the astute signings of giant centre-half Ron Yeats and livewire centre-forward Ian St John transformed the team into the most powerful outfit in the division. The established Roger Hunt instantly clicked with St John and with the new-found strength at the back they were almost unstoppable. At Anfield they were imperious. They had won all six League games this season, scoring 23 and conceding only two. Orient's task this day was immense.

Both sides played to their absolute peak and the result was a game of football that thrilled every one of the 36,612 crowd that day. Leyton Orient lifted themselves onto a plateau that hitherto only Liverpool had reached in the Second Division that campaign, and this plateau was somewhere amongst the gods. The first quarter of the match was a combination of probing attacks in the manner of a boxer jabbing away at his opponent to detect any weaknesses, but then Dave Dunmore opened the game up with a savage punch. He managed the difficult task of nipping past Yeats, but then astonished everyone by smashing in an unstoppable shot from 40 yards that earned a round of applause from the gobsmacked Kop.

Hunt poached an equaliser eight minutes later, but Orient responded with gusto and were back in the lead within a minute. McDonald's corner was aimed towards Foster, who managed to find some space and whip in a quick shot before the defence could respond. Hunt made it 2-2 early in the second half, but it was a howler from George as he allowed Hunt's weak header to fall from his arms and trickle through his legs, though he's certainly not the only keeper to have embarrassed himself in that intimidating amphitheatre.

Many a team would have wilted under the heartache of losing a lead twice there, but Orient still surged forward, aggressively taking the game to Liverpool and this positive approach was rewarded when the tireless Dunmore cracked in a powerful header. The home side immediately came back once more and Tommy Leishman headed in Liverpool's third equaliser of the day.

The drained Orient players filtered into the Supporters Club at the end of the game and were stunned when the Liverpool fans all stood up and gave them a standing ovation and a bout of cheering. They could not believe that a set of rival fans could be that friendly and it provoked a few tears amongst the grateful players. Though Orient slipped down a place in the table, it was an indication that the O's were capable of ascending into the top flight with the right approach, though the middle of the table was very congested with just three points covering eighteen teams at the start of play.

If Orient were to go up, they were given an object lesson in the differences between the two divisions in the League Cup replay at Blackpool. Though they played well, they found no response to two quick goals from Ray Parry, and found themselves 0-5 down when Ray Charnley garnered himself a second-half hat-trick, capped with a superb run through Orient's tattered defence. McDonald did pull a goal back, but the standard of finishing between the two sides was more than a division apart.

Orient did make provision for the future by adding a couple of names to their squad. Harry Gregory was a centre-forward and was rewarded with a professional contract now he had turned eighteen. He had excelled in the Orient youth side and hopes were high for him.

Another schoolboy star was Roger Wedge and Carey snapped him up from Brighton aged just seventeen, before he had even played in their first team. The manager also put in an offer for Fulham's John Doherty, who was able to play as a winger or a striker, but his approach was rebuffed. Rumours abounded that West Ham's reserve keeper Brian Rhodes was also a target, but it was firmly denied. Carey had been told by his directors that money was available for strengthening the team as necessary, but it was certainly the case that the manager was required to be very careful with the funds and there were to be no quick fixes or big-money buys.

CHAPTER THREE

Winning Ways

(November 1961 – February 1962)

There was only one London derby scheduled for Orient in the Second Division this season and the added away support helped lift the attendance inside Brisbane Road on the first Saturday in November to over 13,000 again.

Charlton were at the opposite end of the table to Liverpool, but Orient helped them by playing down to their level. The Addicks' right-back John Sewell had a game to forget as he barged into his own colleague to enable Dunmore to steal in for the opening goal just after the break and then foolishly pulled the ball down with his hand to concede a penalty, which Dunmore greedily converted. Without these errors, Orient may have been in trouble, because Lewis pulled a goal back for the visitors with a neat back-heel just before the end, and then Dennis Edwards missed a golden chance at the death with only George to beat. Orient's right-back Stan Charlton was also hampered because he had been playing with his neck in plaster following the removal of a cyst. The bottom side had won at Derby in the previous game, so were well capable of damaging the O's.

On the Thursday, there was a more relaxed game being played at the McEntee Technical School on Billet Road in Walthamstow. Johnny Carey managed an All-Star side against the school's first eleven, and he picked an eclectic bunch, including Ron Greenwood of West Ham, Trevor Bailey of Essex County Cricket Club (and later a stalwart with BBC radio Test Match Special), and several local amateurs. He also picked himself and his coach Eddie Baily too. A game that was light-hearted and entertaining was won by the All-Stars 5-4.

On the Saturday it was back to the serious business of Division Two and a visit to Leeds United, who were still struggling at the foot of the table under the stewardship of new player-manager Don Revie. One noticeable absentee at the game was Carey, who travelled to Norwich to watch George Waites, who Orient had sold to the Canaries at the beginning of the year.

The O's manager had a long shopping list of players he felt were within his reach, but it was a tough job persuading players that Leyton was the place to be, and convincing clubs that Orient's terms were generous. Patience was required and Orient did manage to capture their targets eventually. It was to be a relatively short wait for Waites, but Brighton's inside-forward Tony Nicholas proved too expensive for Carey, and Orient didn't sign him until 1965. Eddie Thomas of Blackburn was another sought-after inside-forward, but Rovers insisted on a part-exchange deal which Carey wasn't keen on. Thomas eventually turned out in Orient's colours, but not until 1967. Orient's most pressing need was for a centre-forward, but Fulham's England Amateur International Bobby Brown went to Watford instead.

Foster was a rare visitor to Orient's cobwebbed treatment room, so Elwood donned the No 8 shirt in his place. He did OK, but sloppy finishing again let down the O's. Dunmore hit a post and Graham sent a right-foot shot over the bar when maybe he should have hit it with his more reliable left peg. Leeds were incapable of scoring, despite the presence of a teenage Billy Bremner and Orient's first goalless draw for twenty months was the result.

Orient's over-reliance on their one true target man, Dave Dunmore, was illustrated on the following Saturday, when Grant Millard, the *Walthamstow Guardian*'s football correspondent, noted that Orient only played well when Dunmore did. Thankfully, Dunmore was red-hot for this home game against Brighton and the south-coast club were four goals down by half-time. Dunmore snaffled a rebound to open proceedings and utility man Elwood (replacing Graham today) beautifully dipped the ball over the keeper's head for the second. Brighton's defence was anarchic by then and left-back Tony Sitford passed the ball into his own net for the third. He also lost the ball to the effervescent White, who made it four. To their credit, Albion did tighten things up in the second half as Orient switched to auto-pilot and they pulled a goal back through Nicholas – the player Carey was after.

A Friday-night fixture in Scunthorpe wouldn't have excited anyone much at the start of the season, but by 24 November it was a crucial game at the top of the table. Scunthorpe, under manager Dick Duckworth, had surprised everybody by climbing up to second on the back of an unbeaten home record. The Iron had only been League members for eleven years, but were now contenders for promotion to the top flight, just ahead of Orient, but behind the unstoppable Liverpool (who were to beat Swansea 5-0 the following day).

A good crowd of 11,712 turned up at the Old Showground and a corker of a game followed, with both sides attacking with fervour. It's doubtful whether Scunthorpe's prolific striker Barrie Thomas – he was to grab a record 31 goals this season – had ever been so well-marshalled, as Bishop made it his mission to stick close by him for the entire match. With their chief threat nullified, Orient were able to take advantage of a defensive slip-up at the other end, when White teed up McDonald early on. Both sides tested the other's defence throughout the game and the Iron won seven corners in the first twenty minutes after the break, but still Orient remained unbowed and managed to add a second goal from a White shot at the end. The win lifted Orient above the Iron and at the end of Saturday the table looked like this.

	P	Pts
1 Liverpool	19	31
2 ORIENT	19	23
3 Rotherham	18	23
4 Scunthorpe	19	22
5 Sunderland	19	22
6 Derby	19	22

Orient entered December with a home game against mid-table Norwich City and the 13,000 crowd included Britain's most successful singer at the time – Cliff Richard. He wasn't a football fan, but two of Orient's directors just happened to be giants of the theatrical agency scene – brothers Les Grade and Bernard Delfont. Consequently there were a succession of well-known faces appearing in the unlikely environs of Brisbane Road, including other top singers of the day like Frankie Vaughan and Helen Shapiro. Grade and Delfont were friends with Orient's chairman Harry Zussman as they were both part of East London's large Jewish community, though Harry had made his money in the boot and shoe trade, rather than show business.

Neither of the two theatrical impresarios put huge amounts of money into the club, but they did work hard at helping to inject a nice family atmosphere. Les Grade in particular was a regular on the train journeys to away matches and he lifted the morale of the players by giving them nice little bonuses, such as giving them tickets to the top West End shows and Royal Variety Performances.

Given the fact that Orient's players weren't very well paid in comparison with other London clubs, these nice little touches made all the difference. Another familiar sight at the club was the young Michael Grade, who used to pull up in his flash new E-Type Jaguar.

All the entertainment today was provided by Orient, however, and Cliff didn't stand up at half-time and sing his current hit *When The Girl In Your Arms Is The Girl In Your Heart*. Instead it was Dave Dunmore who captivated the audience with a mesmerising performance that pulled the Canaries defence all over the place. Ably supported by the inside-forwards and wingers, who were critical to the supply to Dunmore, the visitors' resolve was gradually ground down. An indirect free-kick provided the opening goal midway through the first half. Lea set up Dunmore and the centre-forward hit a beautifully floated ball into the only portion of the net not guarded by a yellow or green shirt. With the heavy balls used in those days there was no chance to 'bend it like Beckham'.

A big win would have been on the cards today, but a determined reserve goalkeeper and the woodwork both combined to keep the damage down to 2-0, Orient's other goal again coming from Dunmore, this time with a superb run and sizzling shot with fifteen minutes remaining. Orient were not going to give up their hard-won promotion place easily.

Theatre tickets weren't the only perks coming the way of the players and on Monday morning they set off for a four-day break at Broadstairs, with accommodation being provided by F John Young, Orient's president.

The idea behind it was to help tone up their bodies for the critical winter spell ahead, where game after game would take place on muddy waterlogged pitches that sapped the energy. There was nothing too physically demanding: rounds of golf and five-a-side sessions in the gym were enough to keep them fit and provide a nice change from the drudgery of training in East London.

Money matters were still occupying the minds of the board though, and they announced that the club was losing £150 a week – a figure that was mysteriously soon updated to £200 a week. It must have been annoying for the board that attendances hadn't shot up as a result of the team's success; in fact they hadn't really risen at all compared to the end of last season when relegation looked imminent.

Usually clubs like Leyton Orient, which are geographically surrounded by other clubs, do relatively badly when times are hard, but pick up large amounts of support when success is achieved, compared to clubs out in the sticks, whose support remains more constant. This hadn't happened yet, maybe the stay-at-homes were convinced that the success was a flash-in-the-pan that couldn't be sustained and needed more convincing.

Either way, the break-even figure of a 15,000 gate was mentioned again, though Orient still hadn't got within 1,500 of that this season. Again it must be stressed that the new contracts that some players had signed weren't noticeably more generous compared to the days when the maximum wage was in operation, it was only the top First Division stars who really noticed the difference. The only big hike in the wage bill came from all the performance bonuses – £2 a head for a win and £1 for a draw. The O's board weren't used to shelling out for these on a weekly basis!

The O's players were fit and raring to go for the trip up to Bury, so it was a disappointment that the game was called off due to thick fog in Lancashire. When teams are doing well, the matches can't come fast enough as they try to keep the momentum going, but now they had to put up with a fortnight's break from footy. Spare a thought, though, for eighteen-year-old Harry Gregory. He was all set to make his debut at inside-forward in place of the flu-ridden Elwood, but his chance evaporated, unlike the Bury fog.

Carey made a surprise change to the line-up for the mid-December game at home to Newcastle, by bringing in Bill Robertson in goal in place of George. It was Robertson's first game since April and it must have been a nerve-wracking occasion because he had suffered at the hands of Orient's boo-boys in the past and been described, somewhat cruelly, as 'the butt of Brisbane Road'. In many ways George and Robertson were similar characters, quiet and steady, not given to the histrionics of many other keepers.

Occasionally though, Robertson's mild-mannered persona could crack. In a game at Swansea in March, an opponent spent the entire match goading him. The goalie refused to rise to the bait and stoically went about his business, telling the antagonist that he was wasting his time. When the referee's whistle blew at full-time, the Orient players were astonished to see Robertson sprinting off the pitch ahead of them, because he normally walked off. When they reached the tunnel they were confronted by the sight of the Swansea player laid out on the floor, with an innocent-looking Robertson sitting calmly in the dressing room.

Newcastle were languishing in the bottom half of the table, but it seemed as though they were stung with the realisation that these

London upstarts were doing so much better than them. They did their best and attacked with intent, but were firmly repelled by the unflappable Lucas-Bishop-Lea half-back line that was starting to get recognition away from East London. Even when players of the calibre of Ivor Allchurch did manage to break through, they found that Robertson was doggedly determined to preserve a clean sheet at whatever cost, and a couple of certain goals were stopped by the lightning-quick reactions of the man who was playing to keep his place.

Orient, in contrast, bided their time and when the half-chances came their way they took them. Dunmore turned provider after half an hour with a cross that White steered in with his head, and Elwood was the only player on the pitch who didn't stop and wait in vain for the referee's whistle following a 57th-minute foul on Foster. He made it 2-0 – the third consecutive game that had ended with that scoreline. In the days when teams level on points were separated by goal-average (goals scored divided by goals conceded) it was useful to notch up wins whilst preserving a clean sheet.

Despite having just come back from their Kent break, the players sauntered off to Jersey at the expense of chairman Zussman as a thank you for avoiding relegation the previous season, though by this halfway point they were only about six points away from avoiding it this time too!

The chairman had by this time stated that an apparent bid from Leicester for Dave Dunmore had been rebuffed, the figure being offered was rumoured to be £25,000. Dunmore wasn't aware of Leicester's bid, none of the players knew about these rumours unless they were tipped off about scouts in the crowd. Zussman said that none of the star players were for sale, which proved that – even if he wasn't going to splash out on expensive new signings in a bid to buy promotion – at least he wasn't going to cut his losses by selling their assets. Though many of the fans were frustrated about Zussman's reluctance to give Carey a blank cheque, it must be remembered that the chairman was at least ensuring that Orient were on a sound financial footing for the future.

The conservative Carey reinstated George in goal for the visit to Middlesbrough on the Saturday before Christmas, which implies that George was dropped for fitness reasons rather than tactical ones. He did let in a couple of goals on his return, but they were penalties and he could do little about them. Lewis had conceded the first one and these days he would have been sent off for deliberately preventing a certain goal with his hand, but in the 1960s a penalty was deemed to be sufficient punishment and he wasn't even booked. At no time did Boro actually take the lead, they were 0-1 and 1-3 down when Bill Harris dispatched his spot-kicks and they never looked like beating the O's, even though the 3-2 scoreline looks tight. The O's defence kept the home team's attack at bay with its customary confidence, which provided a springboard for Orient's midfield to push forward comfortably and create havoc at the other end. Man-of-the-match was Foster, who decided the match's destiny with a couple of goals either side of half-time, with a header and a shot both set up by White, who was enjoying himself on the right wing. tormenting left-back Mick McNeil – an England international.

Boxing Day traditionally draws a good crowd and 14,500 merry souls wended their way into Orient's ground for the visit of Swansea, the gate being helped by West Ham's generosity. Orient had a good working relationship with their close neighbours, no doubt helped by the fact that the two clubs weren't in direct competition with each other. Usually the two sides wouldn't play home games simultaneously, but the League gave them both home fixtures in the afternoon today. Without being asked, West Ham offered to switch their match to the morning, so as not to clash with Orient's fixture, mindful of the fact that the entourage from Swansea couldn't make it in time for an early kick-off.

Of course it worked slightly in West Ham's favour, because no doubt some fans attended both games, but as the senior club the Hammers could have done what they liked without reference to their lowly cousins. In midweek games, the Hammers usually opted for Monday nights, with Spurs playing on Wednesdays. Orient tended to fit in as best they could, often going for Mondays when the Hammers weren't playing, but sometimes opting for other days too.

Swansea's manager Trevor Morris had obviously asked his players for a Christmas present of aggression, judging by the way they set about the task of quietening down the form team of Division Two, but the O's players wisely countered by outplaying them rather than outfighting them. Dave Dunmore's narrow-angled strike after half-an-hour was what separated the sides on paper but, just like the previous game, in reality there was a comfortable gulf between them. Much credit must go to manager Carey, but he was not an egotist and stated modestly that he didn't teach the players a thing; he merely made the odd suggestion here and there. We can safely assume though, that Carey's 'odd suggestions' were astute observations that were eagerly acted upon by the players.

In those days, the return fixture came immediately, so four days later Orient hopped onto a British Railways train and made their way to South Wales. This tradition ensured that any bad blood between opposition players that had occurred in the first game could be carried through for another hour and a half, but thankfully this was a cleaner game than the previous one, with football taking preference over all-in wrestling. Swansea dominated the possession, but they made little headway when they came up against what appeared to be a solid wall of Orient defenders. The back line had played together so many times that they instinctively covered for each other and positioned themselves to minimise any threat from the opposition, whilst instantly switching to an attacking frame of mind when the ball was won. The defence was only punctured once today, by a brilliant run from Graham Williams who created a goal to make it 1-1, but Orient's finishing was on a higher plane.

The difference was Dunmore. Three years ago, the player had nearly become a Swansea player when a player-swap with Spurs for Welsh international Mel Charles was mooted, but that had fallen through, enabling Orient to capture Dunmore instead. Now he showed exactly what the Swans had missed out on. After eleven minutes he followed up his own blocked shot by sharply heading in the rebound, and then he killed the game off with two powerful shots after frightening the opposition defenders into mistakes.

The inside-forwards Foster and White, and wingers McDonald and Elwood, were happily supplying the hat-trick hero with balls when they could, knowing that not only was he a lethal marksman when given a half-chance, he was also an expert at holding the ball up whilst waiting for support, not something that some selfish strikers were bothered about. The 3-1 win was Orient's seventh consecutive victory and they were now well established in the second promotion place, just two points behind leaders Liverpool (only two went up).

	P	Pts
1 Liverpool	24	35
2 ORIENT	24	33
3 Southampton	25	28
4 Derby	25	28
5 Plymouth	25	28

No matter how much excitement was generated in the Leyton area by Orient's graceful ascent towards Division One, the competition which still held the fans' attention more than any other was the FA Cup, and if a poll had been held, most O's fans would almost certainly have preferred their team to win the FA Cup than gain promotion.

The third round draw gave them an away tie at Third Division strugglers Brentford and the match was originally scheduled for Wednesday, 3 January 1962 with a 3pm kick-off. Orient successfully asked the FA for a switch to 2.15, claiming that the floodlights at Griffin Park were too dim. Brentford complained that the change in times would take £700 off their gate receipts, as some people wouldn't be able to knock off work early, but in the end the match took place on the Saturday anyway, thanks to the weather.

Orient supporters were given 700 stand tickets for the game at 7 shillings (35p) each. With 19,000 home fans also pouring through the turnstiles, the importance of the game is evident, especially combined with the way that Brentford played. The team in red and white stripes forgot about the fact they were almost two divisions below their opponents and gave it everything.

Their positive attitude was rewarded with a goal seconds before the half-time whistle when George Summers poached at a free-kick. Orient didn't deserve any favours for their poor showing, but the Bees' centre-half was crocked early in the second half and was forced to play on the left wing, the customary position for one-legged players. Foster took advantage by equalising after an hour, but then the home side were effectively down to nine men when the goalscorer started limping. Justice wouldn't have been done if the O's had scored a winner, so a retrial was ordered for Monday.

The home game against Swansea had attracted a gate of 14,550, but 22,690 found their way to Brisbane Road for the FA Cup replay, further proof of where the fans' priorities lay. It's a reasonable assumption that many of the extra 8,000 present hadn't seen the O's play since the last home FA Cup-tie eleven months ago, so it was important to put on a good show to encourage them to attend the League games too. Good football was difficult, due to a gale that was blowing down the pitch, but it helped Brentford in the first half and they took the lead from a wind-assisted strike from Tom Higginson.

The wind became Orient's twelfth man in the second half, and once again Foster equalised for the O's, on the hour, though deflecting a ball into the net when you are flat on your back is an unusual method of scoring. Poor Brentford's energy was sapped facing the double onslaught of the weather and their doughty opponents, and gradually the O's wore them down, though they left it late to settle the outcome. Most fans were contemplating a second replay when the tiny figure of Elwood latched onto a weak back-pass from Jim Gitsham to steal the winner.

The FA Cup success did help swell the attendance for Saturday's home League game with Walsall and a 15,000 gate was recorded for the first time in the League since April 1960. Orient's exploits were also now attracting national interest and even *The Times* newspaper deigned to send a reporter to the game. Usually they were more excited by amateur football. Once more Orient faced a strong wind in the first half, but this time the defence held firm until they reaped the benefits in the second. Walsall's best defender had been the woodwork and both posts had been struck and the crossbar rattled twice before Jim Dudley brought down Foster for a penalty. Dunmore tucked his spot-kick away in the corner and Walsall's resolve evaporated.

Ron Newman was on the left wing today, his first League game of the season, in place of the busy Terry McDonald. Newman was a pacy winger, like the man he replaced and he used that ability to beat his man and cross to Graham, whose header doubled his side's advantage three minutes after the penalty. White added a third, though his shot was helped over the line by an embarrassing fumble from keeper Alan Boswell.

Derby County were one of the handful of teams that had been challenging Orient for one of the two promotion places, but who had been left trailing in their wake by the Londoners' eight-match winning sprint. The meeting at the Baseball Ground was therefore critical for the Rams, who desperately needed to close the gap and shake their rivals' sky-high confidence.

The importance of the fixture was not lost on either set of players and the game developed into one of those blood-and-thunder encounters so beloved by the fans, with just the odd flash of skill to remind everyone of the high ranking of both sides. Derby's giant centre-half Les Moore was detailed to take care of Dunmore, and no wonder, because the striker had bagged nineteen goals in 25 League games, including eight in the last six.

Moore set about his task with undue relish and soon the crowd of 22,000 had their eyes glued on the pair as they squared up to each other. Dunmore was the first to suffer when he chased a ball into touch and found himself being propelled towards the edge of the stands by a hard-charging Moore.

Dunmore responded by outwitting his opponent by speed and stealth and he broke away from his marker later on, only to find himself spread-eagled on the cold turf by a crunching tackle that left his thigh feeling like it had been trampled on by a runaway bull. Having failed to get the better of Moore by legitimate means, Dunmore exacted his revenge by a crude hack at Moore a few minutes later, but referee Jack Kelly was keeping a sharp eye on matters and he booked the errant Dunmore for having 'done Moore', though the referee had failed to spot the flying fist of an unrecognised opponent who had flattened Foster almost at the start.

Bill Curry had reminded everybody of the finer points of football by tangoing his way through Orient's defence and giving Derby a seventeenth-minute lead. Orient for once, found it difficult to get back on level terms and somewhat disheartened they trudged into the dressing room for their half-time cup of tea.

Many managers would have ranted at their side under such circumstances, or given the men a welter of confusing orders to try and change things, but that wasn't the style of Carey. He simply told them to carry on playing the way they were, secure in the belief that his men's superior fitness, passing and assurance would overcome the deficit. Coach Baily was much more passionate in his dealings with the players, but he too kept his orders simple, whilst injecting an extra dose of certitude into his charges.

This attitude was repaid by a two-goal spell midway through the second half. Graham had a header handled on the line by Jack Parry, and nobody was going to stop Dunmore from converting his penalty. Dunmore returned the favour seven minutes later by passing to Graham, who joyously let loose with a rocket-shot from the edge of the area. The identity of the scorer was no surprise to the fans, who were familiar with his ability to turn the outcome of a game with an unexpected shot from his trusty left peg.

Carey contentedly puffed at his pipe at the end of the game, but still managed a quote: 'To say I'm pleased with this win would be putting it mildly. This is the most important match we've played this season and the lads came through it brilliantly.'

Carey would have been even more pleased to hear that Liverpool had dropped a point at Scunthorpe to enable his upstarts to get within a point of the Reds. Southampton had beaten Bury 5-3 and were now

Orient's nearest challengers, five points behind, though Rotherham (1-0 winners at Norwich) had two games in hand and were seven points adrift. Orient had now won nine League matches on the bounce and needed just one more to equal the record that they had set on their way to the Division Three (South) championship in 1955-56. They had already matched their record of thirteen consecutive unbeaten League games from seven years ago.

One of the favourite pastimes of the players on the train ride home was to locate a copy of the special editions of the local papers that were miraculously rushed out after the games, like the *Pink 'Un* and the *Green 'Un*. These were often on sale before the players and fans had made it home and were eagerly snapped up by all football fanatics, as very few people had portable transistor radios.

Those who did would tune into the BBC's 'Light' network to hear Sports Report at 5pm. Those still at home who had television sets could pick up the results from the BBC (who only had one channel then) or ITV. They could also watch *Sportsview Football Special* later that night, which was a forerunner of *Match of the Day*, though Orient were extremely unlikely to feature.

One team who did regularly feature were Burnley, the team now sitting proudly atop the First Division, two points clear of Tottenham. Orient were handed the toughest possible draw in the FA Cup fourth round by being given a trek up to Turf Moor for the game on Saturday, 27 January.

In the end it was a longer journey than they feared. Thick fog descended on Lancashire in the early afternoon and the turnstiles at Turf Moor stayed resolutely locked, much to the dismay of the faithful O's fans who were kept outside, foiled by the late postponement of the game. Other matches in the area also suffered and Manchester United's home tie with Arsenal was called off with the crowd already in the ground, whilst Weymouth had held Preston goalless for fourteen minutes before their game was abandoned (they succumbed 0-2 in the replay). Oldham were chuffed that Boundary Park escaped the worst of the fog, despite its close proximity to Manchester, though after they were beaten by Liverpool regretted their brief joy.

Orient did get to play the game on Tuesday, even though the fog had given way to torrential rain. The inclement weather did nothing to deter the 37,932 spectators who turned up, and the atmosphere was crackling with tension. It may be hard for younger readers to comprehend the fact that Burnley were such a big club, but they had been First Division

champions in 1960 and FA Cup semi-finalists the following year. They
had won ten out of their twelve home games in the League this season
and had scored 72 goals in their 24 League games, an average of three
a game. Their forward line of Jim McIlroy, Ray Pointer, John Connelly,
Gordon Harris and Jim Robson gave innumerable defenders sleepless
nights and Orient's famed defence was going to be tested like it never
had been before.

The visitors were at full strength, with Newman giving way to the
more-favoured McDonald on the left wing. Not that McDonald had
always been so well regarded. The lively winger was once walking cheer-
fully towards Brisbane Road when an O's fan stopped him and asked
him if he was playing. When the player replied proudly that he was, he
was soon cut short by the fan's reply as he walked away: 'That's torn it!'
McDonald used the retort as an encouragement, and he turned the
crowd around by using his electric pace to full effect by skinning a succession of right-backs.

Orient's plan was to enlist the help of their midfielders to help the
overworked back line and this worked a treat. Flying wingers Connelly
and Harris were kept quiet by full-backs Charlton and Lewis, and
Bishop stifled much of the danger out of Pointer by his close attention.
McIlroy was the hardest man to handle, but even he found the going
tough against the determined mob from London E10.

With many of Orient's middle men called back for defensive duties,
the forward men relied heavily on the occasional quick breakaway and
their tactics met with spectacular success after 56 minutes. Lea forgot
about his role at the back for once and sprinted up the right wing, sending over a ball to the far side that Graham cleverly nodded into the path
of Foster, who only had to give the ball the lightest of touches to beat
Adam Blacklaw.

Falling a goal behind was the catalyst for a renewed onslaught from
the Clarets, and George was soon over-employed in goal, using hands
and feet to deny the marauding hordes. The very best sides never give
up though, and just like the previous home game when they left it late
to earn a draw, so they did today. Veteran Jimmy Adamson ran down
the pitch and sent an exquisite through ball to Harris who smacked the
ball home.

Orient then had to suffer an anxious seven minutes till the end, but
they earned their replay in a week's time. Adamson later admitted that
Orient 'gave us a scare and I have rarely seen a team fight so hard'.
Orient's captain Charlton was in agreement and said that if they could

fight the same way in the replay, then they had a chance. Carey was proud that his men were one of the 'few teams that can hold Burnley at Turf Moor and the way they did it was magnificent'. Chairman Harry Zussman (with due regard to the accounts no doubt) said he was delighted that 'our own supporters will get a chance to see the match'.

CHAPTER FOUR

Surviving the Jitters

(February-April 1962)

Sandwiched in between the FA Cup saga with Burnley was a reminder of a more realistic chance of Orient covering themselves with glory at the end of the season. It's a thankless task for any manager to exhort his players into forgetting about a forthcoming blockbuster of an FA Cup-tie and to concentrate on a humble League match against lowlier opposition, though. Like young children who are told to concentrate on their homework whilst ignoring the fact there is a great big chocolate cake sitting on the sideboard, players always seem to allow their attention to wander away from the task in hand.

The fact that Orient's opponents for this game were Bristol Rovers added even more elements of danger for the home side. Rovers were next-to-bottom of the Second Division and fighting for survival, but so far below Orient in the table for the conviction to unconsciously enter the players' minds that they could play this game at perhaps four-fifths of their usual work rate and still win.

The other point that should be remembered is that Rovers had already beaten Orient in a League game this season. Dunmore had recovered from his thigh injury and Carey saw no reason to change his winning side, even to rest any players for the Cup game three days hence, but Rovers introduced their new inside-forward Keith Williams, recently purchased from Plymouth Argyle. He was eager to show his new club what he was capable of, and after twenty minutes he astonished everybody by unleashing an almighty shot from distance to open the scoring.

This provoked the home team into some sort of response and five minutes later the dynamic figure of McDonald leapt through the air to deliver his riposte. Ray Mabbutt gave Rovers the lead again, early in the second half, only for Orient to find another equaliser, this time courtesy of Graham. Orient were always chasing the game though, and never seemed to have the conviction to go out and win it. Rovers were more adventurous and when Harold Jarman scored with a dozen minutes remaining, the boys in blue were unable to conjure up a third equaliser.

So the magnificent run of winning and unbeaten games came to an end and eleven weary legs and minds trudged off the heavy pitch with an inkling of self-doubt creeping into the recesses of their brains.

Any physical knocks sustained by the players would have been worked on by trainer Les Gore the following day, but for once Brisbane Road wasn't deserted on a Sunday as tickets went on sale for the titanic replay with Burnley two days later. The ticket office was besieged by people who probably only went to games about once a season, if at all, and no doubt there were dark mutterings from the regulars as they found themselves at the back of a queue of about 22,000 people. A ticket to the West Stand would have cost 3s 9d (just under 19p) and you can almost imagine Harry Zussman watching the scenes and dancing up and down as he puffed on his big cigar, as for once the financial plight of his club was temporarily eased.

Tuesday, 6 February 1962 saw 31,000 people descend on the ground, more than double the number that had attended the previous League match and a further indication of which competition was foremost in people's affections at the time. In theory, another 4,000 could have been shoehorned inside the ground, but even so it equalled the record attendance for Brisbane Road. The 31,000 figure was also recorded in FA Cup-ties against Port Vale (quarter-final, March 1954) and Sheffield Wednesday (fifth round, February 1961). It wasn't a club record though, as three higher attendances had been recorded at Millfields Road, the peak being 37,615 against Spurs in a Division Two game in March 1929.

The Brisbane Road record was set to stand for less than three years, until 34,345 attended the fourth round FA Cup-tie with West Ham – the current (and presumably all-time) benchmark. The receipts for the Burnley game totalled £5,255, which means on average everyone was shelling out the equivalent of seventeen new pence per ticket.

If Burnley had been surprised by Orient's endeavours at Turf Moor, then they could scarcely believe how their opponents could lift their game even higher for the Brisbane Road showdown. Orient felt able to push forward more and Burnley found themselves on the back foot for once. Foster, Graham and Lucas were all denied by a combination of great goalkeeping from Adam Blacklaw and astute positioning from his white-shirted colleagues, blocking anything on the goal-line that beat the man in green.

It was Dunmore though, who terrorised Burnley the most. Tom Cummings had been with Burnley for fourteen years, but it is unlikely that the centre-half had encountered anyone more challenging than the giant, yet extremely mobile figure of menace, and Cummings was having to be backed up by other colleagues in double-marking manoeuvres. A catalogue of half-chances fell to Dunmore and the ball was sent whizzing close to the post each time, though always on the wrong side. This underlines the weakness that was evident today and on frequent occasions during these two featured seasons. Dunmore felt he had to shoot, because of the lack of support that a second recognised striker would have given him.

Burnley received help in the second half from the wind which was now blowing in their favour. After an hour they won a corner which was headed goalwards by Brian Miller. George flapped at it, but could only direct it onto the underside of the corner of the crossbar, where Lewis was stationed just behind the goal-line. He headed it clear, but referee James adjudged that it had clearly crossed the goal-line.

As if this wasn't enough pain for Lewis to endure, it was added to when he collided with the post immediately after heading the ball. The O's had further chances to score, but Burnley somehow managed to cling on to their precious lead. In terms of effort and possession it was floodlight robbery, but Orient never took their numerous chances whereas their opponents clinically accepted one of their rare opportunities – a common footballing tale.

For once, Orient dominated the sports pages of all the daily newspapers (though the fact that this was the only FA Cup-tie played that night helped enormously). There was much sympathy for the losers and a unanimous verdict that Burnley were lucky, an opinion shared by their manager Harry Potts. One unknown individual said that 'it was the greatest robbery since the Cup was stolen in 1895'. It was left to 'Gentleman' Johnny Carey to provide the best summing up, though: 'It's Division One or bust now, lads. You proved tonight that you are a great side, but you just weren't meant to win. Accept this fact and forget the game. Promotion is the only thing that matters now, and I know that you can do it.' It was especially hard on Carey, for the reward for beating Burnley would have been a home game against his former club Everton. Burnley went on to reach the final, when Tottenham ran out 3-1 victors.

Joe Elwood may not have been picked for the FA Cup-tie, but he had his moment of glory when he appeared for the Northern Ireland

Under-23 side against Wales the following night. The slightly-built Elwood, who hailed from Glenavon, had won a 'B' cap against France a couple of years before, but was promoted in this goalless draw at Windsor Park in Belfast. Mal Lucas was set to captain the Welsh side, but it wasn't deemed fair to make him play four matches in seven days, so he was dropped, though he did make a solitary appearance for the Under-23s' against Scotland.

Foster was being mentioned as a possibility for the English Under-23 side, but this ambition was never fulfilled. There was also constant speculation about whether Dave Dunmore had done enough to warrant inclusion in England's World Cup squad in Chile that summer. He too was overlooked, though England manager Walter Winterbottom was interested enough to attend Orient's game at home to Preston on Friday night.

Dunmore did impress, but there seemed little appetite amongst his colleagues for the game, which was won comfortably by Preston 2-0. A large enough remnant of fair-weather fans had remained to lift the crowd to a season's high for a League match of nearly 19,000, but they took out their frustration at referee Harry Horner, who consistently seemed to give decisions against the home side, either bravely or foolhardily. Either way, he was given a police escort off the pitch, because at half-time he was bombarded by missiles from the crowd, though a rubber ball and a collection of orange peel were the most dangerous things that were launched at him.

It was annoying that the casual fans had now seen two defeats, although the Friday game also featured some fans from other local clubs, as well as a few players, like West Ham's Scottish goalie Lawrie Leslie, who often used to cheer on Orient from the stands. The O's regular keeper was also a spectator, as Robertson regained his place in goal from George. The two League defeats had narrowed the gap between the O's and the chasing pack, although Southampton and Plymouth also dropped points on Saturday to leave the table like this.

	P	Pts
1 Liverpool	28	42
2 ORIENT	28	37
3 Southampton	29	34
4 Plymouth	29	33
5 Scunthorpe	27	32
6 Rotherham	27	32

Carey was obviously feeling that his team needed shaking up, and he bought Norman Deeley, a Wolves outside-right for over ten years and winner of two England caps in 1959. Deeley had scored 66 goals for Wolves in his 206 League appearances and was therefore seen as a useful addition to Orient's forward line, though he was versatile enough to slot in on either wing.

Indeed, it was left-winger McDonald who was dropped in order to accommodate Deeley into the side for the visit to Plymouth on Saturday, 17 February. The Devonians were also chasing promotion and this resulted in their biggest home gate of the season so far – over 20,000.

The *Walthamstow Guardian's* reporter stated that before this season Orient were synonymous with poor gates away from home, but now they found themselves an attraction. Though they played with more vigour than they did against Preston, they still found themselves two goals down before Dunmore gave them renewed heart with a goal after 76 minutes. They had chances to equalise, but were profligate once again and slumped to their fourth successive defeat.

There were three changes to the Orient side that travelled up to Stoke the following Saturday, but they were forced and not tactical. Charlton had made 73 consecutive appearances since October 1960, but was forced to miss this one due to a knee injury. His replacement was George Wright, who had been waiting patiently in the reserves all season, having been a regular during the previous four years. White was indisposed on the morning of the match for personal reasons, and Deeley showed off his adaptability by switching to the right wing to replace him, enabling Elwood to operate in his accustomed position on the opposite flank. Graham was crocked, so Foster moved to inside-left, despite not being fully fit himself. Bill Taylor came in at No 8, making his second-ever appearance for Orient, his previous one coming in the last game of last season.

With so many changes to an already demoralised side, and with a rejuvenated Stoke team enjoying a run of seven straight home wins since the return of their old favourite Stanley Matthews, it was a recipe for another defeat, but instead it proved to be a return to their old form.

Orient mixed their usual short-passing with a greater use of the long ball and the Stoke defence was unsettled, especially on their right, where Elwood was wreaking havoc, though he blew three great chances of opening the scoring. Stoke tried to counter by pushing players forward in the second half, but this only exposed them further and a quick pass to Dunmore resulted in a searing 25-yard winner just after the hour mark. Matthews did his best, but even with all his guile he wasn't going to put one over on Lewis, especially now he was 46 years old. The sight of Matthews had doubled Stoke's average attendance since his return, so the crowd of nearly 22,000 was a bonus to the O's as they shared the gate receipts.

Charlton regained his place for Orient's next game on Saturday, 3 March, though Wright was presumably unhappy that he was replaced by a man bearing a heavily strapped knee. The injury hampered Charlton somewhat, as a major part of his game involved haring down the right wing.

This made him one of the pioneers of the overlapping right-back role, though it sometimes caused problems for unsuspecting colleagues. He recalls one game whilst he was at Arsenal, when he passed forwards to his wing-half Alex Forbes and then sprinted past him for the return. Forbes wasn't expecting this and casually back-heeled it to where he thought his right-back still was.

Foster also returned, in place of Taylor, though the near 20,000 home element in the Brisbane Road crowd were at a loss to identify the player in the No 10 shirt. Gordon Bolland had been signed from Chelsea just three hours before the kick-off, which helps explain their confusion.

Bolland was just eighteen and had only played two League games for Chelsea. The lanky inside-forward was sitting in his digs at Fulham when his boss Tommy Docherty rang him up and told him that Johnny Carey had made Chelsea an offer (£4,500) that they had accepted. Though technically speaking Docherty only advised him to accept, he intimated that he had no future at Chelsea, so after talking it over with his colleagues Bolland became an Orienteer. Ironically, Chelsea looked set for relegation to Division Two at the time, with Orient replacing them, so that helped the decision-making process. He moved into a club house at Buckhurst Hill that was almost rent-free, sharing it with the other new boys – Norman Deeley, David Clark (recently signed from Leyton), and the old boy, trainer Les Gore. It was a happy house, full of banter.

Orient had also lost two players. Left-half reserve Dennis Sorrell moved to Chelsea for a reported £9,000 fee, whilst keeper David Groombridge, who had last played in goal in April 1960, retired through injury. He became the new player-coach at Athenian League side Leyton, whilst retaining his job as a sports teacher at a school in Notting Hill Gate.

It was Sunderland who were providing the opposition for Bolland's Orient debut and Deeley's first home game. They were hanging around the fringes of the promotion race, though were hugely handicapped by injuries to Charlie Hurley and the ever-lethal Brian Clough. Not that they appeared to be suffering too much, because they took a third-minute lead, when Willie McPheat beat the bandaged Charlton to the ball and chested it home. The goal was missed by many fans, who left it late to enter the ground and were caught out by thousands more with the same idea.

Orient cranked up the pressure in response to Sunderland's goal, especially down the right, where Deeley was floating in a succession of crosses towards the goal. Indeed it was early in the second half when a slightly misjudged centre completely deceived keeper Jim Montgomery and he could only watch in horror as the ball nestled in the far corner, despite Deeley being near the corner flag at the time. At least the 1-1 draw kept Sunderland from creeping closer to the O's hard-fought second placing, but worryingly, it was the third time in succession that Orient had failed to win at home in the League.

Another Friday night game followed, but this time it was an away match at another rival for promotion – Rotherham. White returned to his customary right-wing slot where he was such a star, even though he smoked like a trooper and looked deceptively unfit. Deeley switched wings, so Elwood was dropped and Taylor came in once more in place of Foster.

Millmoor was a bogey ground for Orient, for they had failed to win on nine previous trips there. This was probably their best chance of ending that sequence, but once more they didn't play as well as they ought to have done and allowed the opposition to pick up points. The defence, for once, was vulnerable, though they were hardly any worse than the players in front of them.

The Merry Millers needed no further encouragement and duly took the lead through Don Weston after half-an-hour, though he had already hit a post before then. Ken Houghton made it 2-0 from a corner-kick with twenty minutes to go, and though Lucas reduced the arrears with a long-range mortar bomb soon afterwards, Orient were unable to find an equaliser, not even when Deeley was presented with a three-yard shot with just the goalkeeper to beat in the final minute. He hit the post.

There was little time to rest because the next game was on Tuesday, 13 March. The players came in for their customary loosening-up session on Monday, with gentle exercises to revive their tired muscles. The trip up to Bury on Tuesday meant they avoided a heavier session that usually took place on that day, when sprints and longer distance work were usually on the cards.

Great store was set by keeping the players fit in those days, essential on the boggy grounds they were encountering by now, that sapped the players' strength so quickly. Les Gore was the taskmaster for the most part on that score, with Eddie Baily and his assistant Joe Mallett concentrating on the football coaching, with Johnny Carey supervising from a distance and just making the odd quiet comment to his trusted allies. Baily's championship-winning pedigree (and the fact he was now 36) led him to concentrate on the more skilful aspects of training like one-twos, and the variety of the sessions prevented the players from getting bored. Orient players were still free on most afternoons, so the snooker sessions continued, though they declined an offer to join a new ten-pin bowling league that was just starting up at the Wanstead Playbowl.

There was more shuffling of Carey's pack as McDonald and Graham returned to the fold, fit once more. Deeley and Bolland changed positions, whilst White was sidelined with a knee injury and Taylor was dropped. Morale was boosted by the return of McDonald especially, and the other players were entertained by his exploits at the bookies, especially when he supplied a winning tip. Once they picked up some extra income from a horse called 'Team Spirit', an apt name to pick, because the O's were thriving on it. McDonald turned a hobby into a career later on when he became a bookmaker himself.

McDonald also proved himself a winner on the pitch, because it was his unexpected shot from 30 yards that separated the two teams, midway through the first half. Either side of that, Orient seemed content to soak up the pressure from the home side, though they were fortunate that Bury's finishing was no better than Orient's had been recently. The 1-0 win helped pull Orient two points clear of Scunthorpe and three points ahead of Plymouth, with all sides having nine games remaining.

Liverpool were racing certainties to land the Second Division title and they travelled down to Orient for the next game. The clash of the top two provoked enormous interest and a crowd of 25,880 swarmed into Brisbane Road, the highest League gate for six years. The crowd figure had been predicted by secretary George Hicks and he advised everyone to get in the ground long before the 3.15 kick-off in order to prevent a repetition of the late surge that had occurred during the last home match.

As is quite common in these eagerly awaited clashes between the big sides, they managed to cancel each other out, though the rock-hard nature of the ground didn't seem to help provide free-flowing football. It was soon apparent that one moment of magic was going to decide the game, and just before half-time Graham provided it. He collected a pass from McDonald, somehow slipped his way past Yeats, the man-mountain, and smashed the ball in from well outside the area for a contender for a goal of the season competition.

With Orient's famed half-back line of Lucas, Bishop and Lea snuffing out Liverpool's forward line of A'Court, Hunt and St John, the match remained at 1-0 in Orient's favour with only ten minutes left. Then came a rare mistake from two of the three O's defenders. Lucas and Lea tried a bit of head tennis in order to clear their lines, but the ever alert A'Court slipped in to level the match. Orient were stunned, but incredibly regained their lead when a free-kick from 30 yards was touched to Lewis, who buried it into the back of the net before Liverpool's new keeper Jim Furnell could react.

The Reds weren't dead though, because Charlton, still handicapped by his bad knee, dallied too long on the ball just before the end and A'Court pinched the ball off him once more and netted his second equaliser of the day.

The 2-2 draw almost certainly ended Orient's title hopes, though O's supporters could point to an injury to Dunmore that had in effect robbed them of their main threat. Speedy Bolland had done his best, but the slender youngster was always going to struggle against the physical might of Yeats. Other results amongst their rivals were mixed. Plymouth and Southampton both won, but Scunthorpe and Rotherham lost.

	P	Pts
1 Liverpool	32	48
2 ORIENT	34	43
3 Plymouth	34	41
4 Southampton	35	40
5 Scunthorpe	34	40
6 Rotherham	32	38

Dunmore was fit again for the shortest away trip of the season to Charlton, so Bolland dropped back to inside-forward and Taylor rejoined the reserves.

With so many teams threatening to overhaul Orient on the final run-in – should there be a reoccurrence of their February woes – there was an understandable urgency amongst the blue-clad visitors to wrap this game up early. As is often the case, one man showed by personal example the way for his teammates to follow. Graham was enjoying plenty of service down the right wing and after twenty minutes he spotted Deeley honing in towards the goal and delivered a pinpoint cross to him that cried out for the superb finish that the new boy provided. Graham was keen to earn himself a chunk of personal glory and in the next attack he ignored the other players and forced his way through the home side's defence and made it 2-0.

The home side weren't prepared to lay down and die though, and less than ten minutes later they halved the deficit with a Brian Kinsey header from a corner. Orient were handicapped throughout the second half by another injury to Dunmore, which turned him into little more than an ornament on the edge of the action, and unsurprisingly his side were under the cosh for most of the remaining time. Charlton the stopper was instrumental in frustrating Charlton the team, but it was his colleague Lea who provoked a storm at the end with some over-zealous tackling, though it was usually Lucas who was regarded as the tougher tackler.

Lea was very vocal on the pitch and this may have helped to spark a stand-off with John Hewie and some unseemly jostling and shoving amongst the other players that turned the pitch into a primary school playground. The 2-1 win pushed Orient a little bit closer to promotion, as with only seven games to go there was less and less time for the following clubs to make up the points.

The Essex Professional Cup didn't distract the O's for too long, as a side mostly made up of reserve players succumbed to a 1-2 home defeat at the hands (or rather feet) of Southend in the semi-finals, though it took extra-time for the Shrimpers to prevail. Orient were exempted from the earlier rounds, as befitted their Division One club-in-waiting status.

The injury to Dunmore proved to be too much for the daily attentions of Les Gore's magic sponge, so Orient reverted to their line-up that had earned a draw with Liverpool for the home game against Leeds on the last day of March.

Whilst Dunmore's knock wasn't deemed to be too serious, there was grimmer news concerning Phil White, who had just undergone a cartilage operation at Charing Cross Hospital and was unavailable for the rest of the season.

He was certainly missed by the O's fans, as he would surely have managed to provide more entertainment than the other 22 players on the pitch, because it was a stinker. Obviously all the new fans who had been won over by the Burnley and Liverpool games had somehow been tipped off about this, because the attendance halved, back to the 13,000 hardcore of supporters.

Leeds had just splashed out on Bobby Collins from Everton, but the irrepressible Scottish inside-forward was as subdued as everyone else today, though he would prove to be a key figure in United's resurgence in the mid-1960s. It's interesting to speculate that had Orient managed more than a couple of dismal goalless draws against the Peacocks, manager Don Revie might have had to haul his side up from the Third Division, if he'd lasted that long.

Orient actually closed the gap on leaders Liverpool, who lost at Luton, but Plymouth and Sunderland were closing fast, especially the latter, who were the form team of the division. The three teams immediately below the Rokerites all lost today.

	P	Pts
1 Liverpool	35	52
2 ORIENT	36	46
3 Plymouth	36	45
4 Sunderland	36	42
5 Scunthorpe	36	41
6 Southampton	37	40
7 Rotherham	35	38

The reasonably mild winter had given most teams a fairly gentle run-in, with those clubs who had been knocked out of cups in the earlier stages just having to play Saturday games for the most part. And so it was for Orient, who nipped down to the seaside for a bracing run-in with Brighton.

Orient had four teams in action this season, with the reserves playing midweek games in the Football Combination, the 'A' team appearing in the Seanglian League, and the Colts turning out in the Forest Youth League. One regular for the reserves was called up for a bit of first-team action and that was David Clark, who became the first player of the season to appear in the No 3 shirt, other than its usual wearer Eddie Lewis, who had pulled a muscle. In fact, Les Gore was kept especially busy, with Dunmore's pulled knee muscle and keeper George's painful instep which prevented him kicking. Poor Gore was now working seven days a week, in contrast to the lack of action in the treatment room in the early part of the season.

David Clark was usually found playing the role of a centre-half for the reserves, so it can't have been easy for him, making his first-team debut in a slightly unfamiliar role, though he was given an easy time by his opposing right-winger Mike Tiddy. Clark was born in Leyton and had played for Leyton in the Athenian League, until Carey promoted him into the area's senior side.

He certainly did no worse than many of his more experienced colleagues, because it was another largely lacklustre performance. It was just as well that the deadlock was broken as early as the twentieth minute, though the goal had an element of farce about it. Deeley whipped in a hard low cross from the right and Bolland had a crack at goal which keeper Charlie Baker parried. The ball fell to McDonald who smacked it back towards goal, but Baker again managed to push the ball away.

Finally the ball came to Foster, just back in the side after an injury, who showed his mates just how to smack home an unstoppable volley. At the other end, Robertson too was having problems and just after the interval he fell backwards into the goal following a cannonball shot from Joe Caven though, much to the anger of most of the 13,000 crowd, the referee declared that the ball had not crossed all of the goal-line.

Johnny Carey summed up the attitude of the club during the run-in: 'We are concentrating on teamwork, which brought us our early success. The lads are hard at it every Saturday, so during the week we try to relieve the tension.'

The heavier grounds of the winter months and the strain of so many of the team playing in virtually every game were having an impact on mental and physical fitness, so no wonder Carey was easing their workload, whilst trying to recreate the positive feeling that was evident from the start of the season. The manager himself took his mind from the Division Two closing stages by taking charge of the Republic of Ireland side that played Austria, inspiring his new team to a 3-2 win in Dublin. Carey himself had been an Eire player for eight years, but once missed an international when he insisted on putting his club before his country.

Further international recognition for an Orienteer came on the Wednesday, when Mal Lucas made his Welsh debut. He took the place of Villa's Vic Crowe in the half-back line and put in a competent display, though the Welsh defence was spectacularly unstressed in the 4-0 victory over Northern Ireland at Cardiff. Mel Charles of Cardiff City scored all the goals.

Saturday brought a return to Division Two matters and a clash between the two surprise packages of the promotion fight, Orient and Scunthorpe. Lewis and Dunmore were timely returnees for this big clash, with the inexperienced Clark and Bolland losing their first-team status for now.

Disappointingly it was one of the veterans of the side who made a fatal mistake in the game, and right from the kick-off too. The saying 'he who hesitates is lost' could well have been coined especially for match reports, and the new Welsh international Lucas dithered whilst in possession of the ball, changing his mind and sending his speculative pass to an opponent – John McGuigan, who instantly created a goal for John Kaye that was timed at nine seconds. The Lucas lapse seemed to infiltrate the minds of all of his colleagues and though they enjoyed the majority of the possession, they never showed any of the killer instinct that promotion sides must display and they were unable to equalise.

Orient's mediocre home form was now threatening their promotion chances and the fans had endured five miserable League defeats at Brisbane Road. Thankfully, Plymouth also succumbed to a home defeat (against Bury); otherwise they would have moved into Orient's second-place spot which they had jealously guarded for nearly five months. Sunderland were now racing up on the blind side with another victory (at Luton), whilst Southampton's win dealt a possibly fatal blow to their opponents Rotherham in the battle of the outsiders.

Easter fell late in 1962, so the sequence of three games in four days was going to leave Orient with only one more game to come, so it was crucial for the promotion chances of all of the potential First Division candidates. Liverpool's place in the top flight was almost assured and it was going take a catastrophic collapse to deny them the championship as well. Orient fans were praying that they could emerge into the post-Easter period still in second place, as they definitely didn't want to rely on other results to go their way.

Only the first of these three games was a home encounter, which was perhaps no bad thing, given their poor record on their own patch. Luton were the visitors and one of a plethora of clubs compressed into mid-table with only a tiny number of points separating them. Although promotion was out of the question for these teams, there were still nearly half the teams in the division still nervous about the prospects of others nearer the bottom putting on a spurt to safety, so the Hatters weren't going to take it easy.

A combination of the Easter holiday and a realisation amongst the casual fans that Orient were on the verge of something special boosted the support to over 21,000. They witnessed a typical home game: plenty of possession from their blue-shirted boys and much of it in the opposition half too, but a frustrating lack of clinical efficiency when it came to putting the ball into the onion bag.

The effervescent little livewire that was Norman Deeley was guilty of missing the most chances, though Dunmore was unusually subdued. Perhaps the crowd must take some of the blame, because even regular supporters noted that they were a quieter set of fans than was seen at many clubs, and there was a noticeable absence of singing to spur on the team to greater efforts.

Of course, the 21,000 present today generated a lot of volume, but the encouragement was mixed with an understandable tension as their team's efforts were constantly thwarted. What was needed was the footballing equivalent of Epsom salts, but there was no one to dispense them. McDonald did manage to relieve the tension briefly after the interval when he netted, but the referee and linesman agreed that Dunmore was offside and interfering with play as he attempted to head in his rebounded shot. The crowd's anger boiled over at this latest 'injustice' and the officials were subjected to a bombardment of orange peel for a few minutes.

The match petered out into another goalless draw and it was now seven home games without a win. Of their twenty home games they had won only half, with five defeats, barely any better than the teams at the bottom. There was nothing wrong with their away form, which was the best in the division, but only a tiny number of O's fans ventured away in those days, so the home form was costing them potential regular support from the curious occasionals.

Scunthorpe were the only other top team to play today and their victory effectively ended Southampton's faint hopes of promotion, making it a five-horse race.

	P	Pts
1 Liverpool	36	53
2 ORIENT	39	49
3 Scunthorpe	39	47
4 Sunderland	38	46
5 Plymouth	38	45

The very next day Orient hopped on the Norwich-bound train, but seemed reluctant to board the metaphorical one heading for promotion, because there was another complete absence of goals, as two sound defensive teams kept out the laughably bad finishing abilities of the attackers.

Elsewhere, Liverpool's 2-0 home victory over Southampton confirmed their promotion back to Division One after eight years of near misses, whilst Sunderland moved ominously into third place with a comprehensive 3-0 success over Newcastle. The Rokerites were now just two points behind Orient with a game in hand. Their red-hot form had ignited the attentions of the locals and the crowd figure of nearly 58,000 was the highest of the day in any division. Scunthorpe didn't play, but Plymouth's defeat at Brighton knocked them out of the running for that crucial second-place spot.

Easter Monday saw the return fixture with Luton, but when the Hatters went into an early lead, and Dunmore missed a penalty, the loyal visiting supporters feared they were witnessing the funeral service for their dreams of top-flight football.

Luckily Carey had made a vital change to the line-up that made all the difference. He had tried Taylor for a couple of games at inside-right, but dropped him in favour of Gibbs, who was now fit after suffering a knee injury. The returning Gibbs volleyed Orient level after half an hour, the team's first goal in nearly seven hours of football. He put his side into the lead early in the second half with a header and then was involved in Orient's third goal – a clever free-kick routine which was eventually slammed in by Lucas from distance. Luton tried to fight back, almost literally judging by their vigorous challenges, but Orient's famed defence was unyielding.

Liverpool's home win over Stoke gave them the championship, but of more concern was Sunderland's 4-0 home thrashing of Rotherham, which meant that if they continued their astonishing form and won their last two games, then Orient would need to win as well. Then it would be down to goal-average to decide which team went up.

Although Sunderland's goal-average was superior to Orient's, the peculiarities of that system favoured the team with the best defence – Orient (the fact that it favoured strong defences was one reason why goal-average was eventually abandoned in the 1970s and replaced by goal-difference, which also had the benefit of being much easier for everyone to calculate).

It was now critical for both teams to ensure that not only did they win their games, but they did so whilst keeping a clean sheet. Scunthorpe also won today, but their chances of promotion were now extremely slim, though Plymouth were out of contention.

	P	W	D	L	F	A	Pts	G Ave
1 Liverpool	38	25	7	6	92	36	57	2.555
2 ORIENT	41	21	10	10	67	40	52	1.675
3 Sunderland	40	21	8	11	81	49	50	1.653
4 Scunthorpe	40	21	7	12	84	64	49	1.313

The very next day, Sunderland travelled to Yorkshire for their return fixture with Rotherham. The Merry Millers held on gamely for 68 minutes until Brian Clough struck twice and Charlie Hurley once, to earn a 3-0 victory. It was the worst-possible result from Orient's perspective and they now fell out of the promotion place they had held since November as their North-Eastern rivals boosted their goal-average. Scunthorpe were beaten tonight to finally end their challenge, whilst Liverpool drew.

	P	W	D	L	F	A	Pts	G Ave
1 Liverpool	39	25	8	6	92	36	58	2.555
2 Sunderland	41	22	8	11	84	49	52	1.714
3 ORIENT	41	21	10	10	67	40	52	1.675

Johnny Carey somehow managed to put all of the tension out of his mind on Wednesday evening, because he delivered a lecture to the Irish Olympic Council on 'Fitness for Football'. Also on the platform that night was the legendary American athlete Jesse Owens, who had broken five world records (and equalled another) on one day in 1935, and garnered four Olympic gold medals in Berlin the following year to the disgust of Adolf Hitler. Whether Owens was able to offer Carey any insights into how to pip your footballing rivals at the finishing line isn't recorded.

At least Carey had the support of his chairman, and the affable Mr Zussman said he wasn't bothered if Orient failed to win promotion; it was still his intention to throw a big party for his boys. This remarkable attitude from the man who had run the club for the past fourteen years demonstrates the warm family spirit that flowed through the club. Zussman realised that Carey had achieved a near-miracle to get the team this close and he wasn't going to rant and rave if the dream remained unfulfilled.

The wily Zussman still had a string to pull though, and he picked up the phone and rang the Swansea manager Trevor Morris. The Welsh club were at home to Sunderland for this deciding game and Zussman was concerned that the Swans might take it easy as they had nothing to play for. Zussman promised Morris a new hat if Swansea got a result against Sunderland, to which Morris retorted that it was worth at least a new suit. Zussman agreed and Morris now exhorted his team to one last effort.

Orient had the task of beating Bury at Brisbane Road and Carey made only one change to his side, dropping Foster in favour of Graham. A very disappointing crowd of 21,617 turned up for this fixture, obviously a large percentage of fair-weather supporters didn't believe that Orient were capable of getting a better result than Sunderland.

For the fans that did turn up, access to a transistor radio was essential and the local electrical retailers had done a roaring trade in the new-fangled little sets. The reliance on outside news caused considerable confusion for the players, because they were unaware of what was happening at Swansea, and were therefore mystified by the various groans and cheers that emanated from the crowd, that bore no relation to what was happening on the Brisbane Road pitch. For all concerned it was a roller-coaster of a day, with Mal Graham's goal after fourteen minutes leading to a dramatic release of tension as he headed in Gibbs' flick off Dunmore's cross.

Then came news of a goal for Sunderland, which brought the O's fans back to reality at the half-time interval. Soon after the break there was another eruption round the ground as Swansea's equaliser was broadcast. The players guessed what had happened, but far from reassuring them, it made them more nervous as it dawned on them that the future of the club was back in their hands once again. This was evident as several good chances were spurned, with Bury's Chris Harker seeming to be on a one-man mission to stop the O's from scoring again –

somewhat curious as the Bury keeper had once been a Newcastle player, the arch-rivals of Sunderland.

Even more strangely, it was Harker who was destined to effectively end the career of Sunderland's goal machine Brian Clough in an accidental collision in their Boxing Day clash. Bury's Bob Stokoe had reckoned that Clough was play-acting that day, and it was he who now made a fatal mistake for the second goal, also scored by Graham, with six minutes remaining.

Ironically, Stokoe, who had caused so much agony to Sunderland fans with his mistake, later gratified them by taking them to an FA Cup final win in 1973. Graham's left-footed shot from fifteen yards led to a pitch invasion from the younger elements of Orient's support, but the older fans were still staying on the terraces with one ear clamped to their radios, fearful of another Sunderland goal. Eventually the news came through that the match at Swansea had finished 1-1 and Orient's promotion to the First Division was confirmed.

The players somehow managed to leave the pitch and make their way up to the directors box, where they surveyed the incredible scenes of jubilation below them. Lucas remembers that the fact that his side were now in the top flight never sunk into him at the time, not helped by the fact that he never received any medal from the Football League for his achievement (only champions Liverpool were awarded them). Graham, in contrast, was in tears because 'I was so happy for the lads. When you play my kind of game, you've got to score goals, and there's no game I'd rather score in.' It was a personal triumph for the man who had been the subject of intense personal criticism from certain O's fans in previous games.

One other man who was overjoyed was Swansea's manager Trevor Morris who subsequently walked into a local tailors and purchased their best suit. He sent the bill to Harry Zussman who was delighted to pay up. The chairman had stated that his team's promotion had made him 'the happiest man in football'.

The players took part in a long-arranged two-match tour in Holland, but flew back on 12 May for a Celebration Dinner at Plantation House, Mincing Lane, Bishopsgate. This was organised by the Supporters Club for the players, their wives, the directors, the coaches and the administration staff.

Two days later, on the Monday, they had a Civic Reception at Leyton Town Hall as the guests of Leyton Borough Council, which gave the fans another chance to salute their heroes. Later on, the club gave the players a holiday in Majorca, all except Graham that is. He had missed all the celebrations because he was in South America with the Welsh squad. He at least did get to watch the mighty Brazil twice, just prior to their second successive World Cup triumph, though he didn't play.

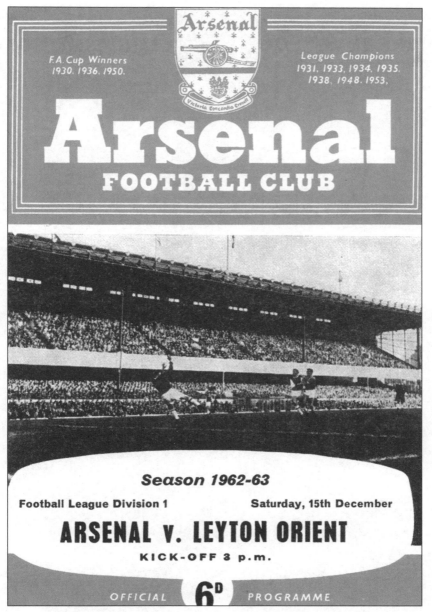

The Big Time is here for Orient, a visit to Highbury in December 1962.
Orient lost 0-2

NORMAN DEELEY having some unluck not to connect with McDONALD'S centre in a recent home game against Scunthorpe.

Norman Deeley looks more like a goalkeeper than a forward in this pose against Scunthorpe in April 1962. Orient lost 0-1

Bury are beaten, Orient are promoted, and the players celebrate in the communal bath (April 1962)

JOHN CAREY, right-back, Manchester United, capped for Ireland 7 times. John is considered the best individual full-back in the game. Here he is timing a header to perfection.

Doctoring photographs is nothing new. This image, half-photo, half-comic strip, shows Orient manager Johnny Carey in his Manchester United playing days

DAVID DUNMORE watches his great effort going inches over the Bury crossbar, with the Bury defence looking on helplessly.

Picture by Stratford Express

The local newspaper highlights goalmouth incidents as Orient beat Bury 2-0
(April 1962)

Dave Dunmore puts Orient 2-1 up at St Andrews in August 1962. Birmingham hit back
to equalise in the second half, denying the O's their first win in Division One

The official envelope of the Leyton Orient Supporters Club

The Orient team are about to take on Everton at Brisbane Road in September 1962.
They are smiling here, but not for long, as Everton won 3-0

The Orient fans invade the pitch after beating Bury to celebrate promotion to the top
division for the first time in the club's history (April 1962)

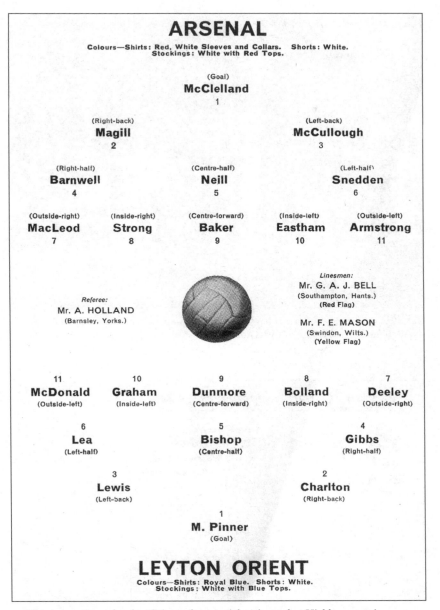

ARSENAL

Colours—Shirts: Red, White Sleeves and Collars. Shorts: White.
Stockings: White with Red Tops.

(Goal)
McClelland
1

(Right-back)
Magill
2

(Left-back)
McCullough
3

(Right-half)
Barnwell
4

(Centre-half)
Neill
5

(Left-half)
Snedden
6

(Outside-right)
MacLeod
7

(Inside-right)
Strong
8

(Centre-forward)
Baker
9

(Inside-left)
Eastham
10

(Outside-left)
Armstrong
11

Referee:
Mr. A. HOLLAND
(Barnsley, Yorks.)

Linesmen:
Mr. G. A. J. BELL
(Southampton, Hants.)
(Red Flag)

Mr. F. E. MASON
(Swindon, Wilts.)
(Yellow Flag)

11
McDonald
(Outside-left)

10
Graham
(Inside-left)

9
Dunmore
(Centre-forward)

8
Bolland
(Inside-right)

7
Deeley
(Outside-right)

6
Lea
(Left-half)

5
Bishop
(Centre-half)

4
Gibbs
(Right-half)

3
Lewis
(Left-back)

2
Charlton
(Right-back)

1
M. Pinner
(Goal)

LEYTON ORIENT

Colours—Shirts: Royal Blue. Shorts: White.
Stockings: White with Blue Tops.

This is how it used to be. Orient take on mighty Arsenal at Highbury, not in a cup competition, but in the top division of the Football League (December 1962)

Malcolm Graham takes the congratulations of teammates after scoring against Bury.
With Sunderland failing to win, Graham's two goals clinch promotion (April 1962)

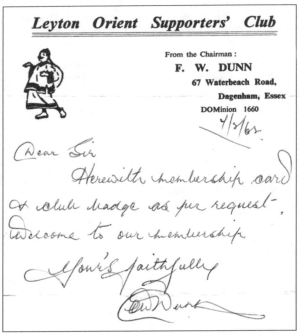

A letter on official
paper from the Leyton
Orient Supporters Club

DIVISION II

	P	Home			Goals		Away			Goals		Pts
		W	D	L	F	A	W	D	L	F	A	
Liverpool	39	17	3	0	66	18	8	5	6	26	18	58
Sunderland	41	17	3	1	60	16	5	5	10	24	33	52
Leyton O.	41	10	5	5	32	17	11	5	5	35	23	52
Scunthorpe	41	14	4	3	52	26	7	3	10	33	41	49
Plymouth A.	41	12	4	4	43	27	7	4	10	30	45	46
Huddersfield	41	11	5	4	39	19	5	7	9	28	37	44
Southampton	41	12	3	5	48	27	5	6	10	24	34	43
Stoke City	41	13	4	4	34	17	4	4	12	20	35	42
Newcastle U.	41	10	5	5	40	24	5	4	12	24	31	39
Charlton A.	40	10	5	6	38	30	5	4	10	30	41	39
Norwich C.	41	10	6	5	36	28	4	5	11	24	40	39
Rotherham	41	9	6	6	36	30	6	3	11	31	46	39
Bury	41	9	4	8	32	36	8	1	11	20	38	39
P.N.E.	41	10	4	6	32	23	4	6	11	21	34	38
Middlesbro'	41	10	3	7	43	28	5	4	12	31	43	37
Luton T.	41	11	1	8	42	37	5	4	12	25	34	37
Walsall	41	10	7	3	38	22	3	4	14	28	52	37
Derby Cty.	41	9	7	4	40	27	4	4	13	26	48	37
Leeds Utd.	41	9	6	6	24	19	2	6	12	23	42	34
Swansea T.	40	9	4	6	33	27	2	7	12	23	53	33
Bristol Rvrs.	41	11	3	7	36	31	2	4	14	17	48	33
Brighton	41	7	7	7	24	32	3	4	13	18	52	31

THE SEANGLIAN LEAGUE

	P	W	D	L	F	A	Pts.
Leyton Orient "A" ...	17	13	1	3	56	17	27
Ashford Town Res. ...	16	12	1	3	54	20	25
Canterbury City Res. ...	18	12	1	5	37	37	25
Margate Res.	17	9	3	5	45	29	21
Dover Res.	16	9	2	5	44	29	18
Gillingham Res. ...	15	6	5	4	34	22	17
Folkestone Town Res. ...	14	6	3	5	31	27	15
Hastings United Res. ...	17	5	3	9	27	41	13
Tunbridge Wells Res. ...	17	4	5	8	22	47	13
Ramsgate Res.	17	3	4	10	29	48	10
Gravesend & N. Res. ...	17	1	6	10	17	48	8
Sittingbourne Res. ...	19	1	4	14	29	61	6

The Division Two league table before Orient's final match against Bury.
Orient not only topped the Seanglian League,
they were also second in the Football Combination, with games in hand

```
                        LEYTON ORIENT FOOTBALL CLUB.
SATURDAY 20TH. OCTOBER 1962.                          KICK-OFF 3-00pm.
FOOTBALL COMBINATION 1961-62 CHAMPIONSHIP.

LEYTON ORIENT(Blue)              v.       TOTTENHAM HOTSPUR(White)
Champions Mid-Week Section                Champions Saturday Section.

M. FINNER                   Goalkeeper           HOLLOWBREAD
RUSSELL                     Right back           BARTON
DEEKS                       Left back            DENNIS
J. PAYNE                    Right half           SMITH   J.
CLARK                       Centre half          SHARPE
GREGORY                     Left half            MARCHI
WHITE                       Outside right        POSSEE
FOSTER                      Inside right         FIFER
WEDGE                       Centre forward       SMITH   R.
ELWOOD                      Inside left          CLAYTON
McDONALD                    Outside left         DYSON

Referee:- Mr. G. W. Davis       Linesmen:- Mr. G. F. Keep
                                           Mr. I. C. Mathews
```

The Football Combination Championship trophy will be presented after the match by Mr. R. H. Pratt(Chairman of The Football Combination)

We would like to welcome players and officials of Tottenham Hotspur Football Club, and offer our congratulations of their achievements over recent years.

The programme for next week it is hoped will contain photographes and autographs of both teams.

IT IS ESSENTIAL THAT SPECTATORS REFRAIN FROM ENCROACHING ON THE FIELD AT ALL TIMES. THIS PRACTICE COULD RESULT IN THE CLOSURE OF THE GROUND. WE APPEAL TO OUR OLDER SUPPORTERS TO HELP US IN STOPPING THE YOUNGER ENTHUSIASTS FROM INVADING THE PLAYING AREA.

SUPPORTTERS CLUB NOTES.

Winning numbers for the Deveopment Pool for the week 15thOct/20th.Oct.

Day		Number		Number	
Monday.	15th October	14812	(£20)	14012	(£5)
Tuesday	16th October	00768	(£20)	07310	(£5)
Wednesday	17th October	00149	(£20)	08719	(£5)
Thursday	18th October	12018	(£20)	09414	(£5)
Friday	19th October	02765	(£20)	01175	(£5)
Saturday	20th October	13501	(£20)	08647	(£5)

Owing to the heavy demand for tickets for the above pool, it is anticipated that a further pool, will start as soon as tickets can be obtained from the printers, the name for this pool will be known as the'Improvement Pool'.

The official paperwork for Orient's home game against Tottenham in the Football Combination Championship (October 1962)

It is October 1962, and Orient stars Bolland, Gibbs, Robertson and Waites
look no different to other healthy, young working men of the time

The association between football and tobacco, as in this Football Fixtures Calculator
from 1962-63, would not be allowed today

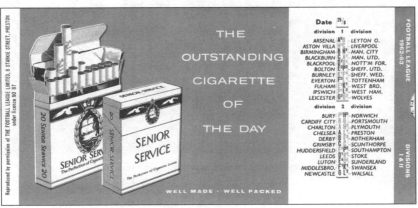

Gordon Banks takes the ball under pressure from Gordon Bolland, with
Frank McLintock in attendance, during the 0-1 FA Cup home defeat by Leicester
(March 1963)

Orient's first match in their 1961-62 promotion season was at Newcastle United. The Magpies programme states St James' Park's capacity. The game ended 0-0. (August 1961)

Where is he now? This young lad is one of the first on the pitch as
the final whistle signals Orient's promotion to Division One in April 1962

The Orient match programme
for the promotion game
against Bury, April 1962. The
front cover was the same for
all matches at that time.
Manager Johnny Carey was
seldom seen without his pipe

DAVID DUNMORE finding the going hard against the 'Wednesday', the centre being brilliantly saved by RON SPRINGETT with his skipper KAY in close attendance.

Orient No 9 Dunmore is squeezed out against Sheffield Wednesday at Brisbane Road.
Orient lost 2-4 in a bad-tempered game. (September 1962)

The Leyton Orient team line-up 1959-60.
Some of these players would be playing in Division One a few years later

Stan Charlton is carried aloft as Orient confirm promotion (April 1962)

Orient's courageous Captain, STAN CHARLTON being carried
from the field by jubilant, admiring fans.

Newspaper images of the Orient clash with the Owls in September 1962

Newcastle United

Colours –Shirts : Black and White Stripes   Shorts : Black

Hollins
(Goal)

2
Keith
(Right-back)

3
McMichael
(Left-back)

4
Neale
(Right-half)

5
McGrath
(Centre-half)

6
Dalton
(Left-half)

7
Hughes
(Outside-right)

8
Harrower
(Inside-right)

9
McGuigan
(Centre-forward)

10
Allchurch
(Inside-left)

11
Tuohy
(Outside-left)

Referee :
Mr. L. J. HAMER,
Bolton.

Linesmen·
Mr. W. R. Dove, Ferryhill.
Yellow Flag

Mr. A. Baldwin, M'brough.
Red Flag

McDonald
(Outside-left)
11

Graham
(Inside-left)
10

Dunmore
(Centre-forward)
9

Foster
(Inside-right)
8

White
(Outside-right)
7

Lea
(Left-half)
6

Bishop
(Centre-half)
5

Lucas
(Right-half)
4

Lewis
(Left-back)
3

Charlton
(Right-back)
2

George
(Goal)

Colours—Shirts : Blue   Shorts : White

Leyton Orient

Band of 105 Corps Eng. Regt., Tyne Elec. Eng. (TA) by kind permission of Lt.-Col. A. K. Johnson, M.B.E. T.D.

Newcastle United's match programme features the local beer in this match,
which ended 0-0 (August 1961)

The Orient eleven that beat Bury to secure promotion to Division One (April 1962)

Orient match programme for the visit of Manchester United, September 1962. The O's won 1-0

The Leyton Orient 1960-61 squad in an informal photograph

Graham makes it 1-1 at Birmingham in August 1962. The game ended 2-2

MALCOLM GRAHAM scoring the first goal against Birmingham.

18-year-old Gordon Bolland before his Orient debut, at home
to Sunderland in March 1962. The game ended 1-1

David DUNMORE (inside forward)

Born at Whitehaven, previous service with York City, Tottenham Hotspur, West Ham, transferred from West Ham 16th March, 1961. Height, 5 ft. 10 ins. Weight, 13 st. 11 lbs.

LEYTON ORIENT SUPPORTERS CLUB

MEMBER'S CARD

Season ...1964/65...
No. ...1867...
Date. ...7/2/62...
Mr. Mrs. Miss Jnr. ...D. Brock...
Membership Sec.
A. DUNN,
67 Waterbeach Road,
Dagenham, Essex
Phone: DOM 1660

Issued subject to Rules. Please quote Membership No. in all correspondence

---

LEYTON ORIENT SUPPORTERS CLUB

MEMBER'S CARD

No. ...479...
Season 1962/3
Date. ...22/6/62...
Mr. Mrs. Miss Jnr. ...D. Brock.
25. Coronation Ave
Stoke. Newington -
London - N.16.
Membership Sec.
E. W. BROCKWELL,
9 Ruckholt Close,
Leyton, E.10
Phone: LEY 3091

Issued subject to Rules. Please quote Membership No. in all correspondence

If you owned one of these, it conferred membership of Leyton Orient Supporters Club

Bury keeper Chris Harker in the thick of it, but he can't prevent
Orient winning 2-0 to gain promotion (April 1962)

**RON NEWMAN
LEYTON ORIENT**

Ron Newman played two games for Orient at outside-left in their promotion season.
Both were in January 1962, and both were won

CHAPTER FIVE

Mixing it with the Big Boys

(August-October 1962)

Orient's promotion to Division One caused much excitement within the club, but also generated a great many problems for it to overcome. Immediately their ascendancy had been confirmed, applications for season tickets flooded into Club Secretary George Hicks' office. Usually there was just a trickle of interest, with regular season ticket holders having their forms dealt with during June, but now the 1,500 season tickets tentatively offered already had potential customers lined up. This was despite a hike in prices, too. Centre-stand seating tickets were now £9 9s (£9.45) with wing seats priced at £8 (an increase of a third). Stand seats for each game were priced at 8s 6d (43p) and 9s 6d (48p) respectively.

Chairman Harry Zussman was predicting average gates of 20,000, with the 31,000 capacity likely to be reached for the visit of clubs like Spurs, Arsenal, Manchester United, Wolves and Burnley. Initially, Zussman indicated that the barest minimum was going to be spent on the ground (six new turnstiles) and that the manager was going to be given a modest amount of money to strengthen the team. Within a week, the chairman had changed his mind, citing the increase in the number of season ticket sales as a reason for this decision. In addition to the already promised new turnstiles at the Buckingham Road end, the club chose to extend the main stand during the close season, resulting in 910 new seats, for which they could charge a premium rate, compared with the terraces.

The cost of the new stand extension was reckoned to be £10,000, but a third of the money was already there through the season ticket sales. This inevitably meant less money was available for manager John Carey to strengthen the team, a factor that was to have a crucial impact on Orient's season in the big time. No doubt many were hoping for a serious investment from the Grade family, but they were concentrating on their show business activities and not looking to squander heaps of cash on football.

There is an old adage about the best way to make a small fortune running a football club, and that's to start with a large fortune. The Grades understood this instinctively and carried on with their morale-boosting activities and behind-the-scenes spending which the players appreciated so much. Though the ground was looking a little less shabby, things weren't exactly plush behind the scenes. Carey didn't have his own office, merely a desk in the boardroom, and he never had his own secretary either. He soon became as skilful in front of a typewriter as he had been on the pitch.

The average age of the first-team squad was 27, which was on the high side, but further study of the ages of the players reveals that the majority of them were either 27 or 28 – namely Bishop, Deeley, Dunmore, George, Gibbs, Graham, Lea and Lewis. These players were probably at their peak and their abilities would presumably start to decline over the next few seasons, which pointed to some major team rebuilding ahead.

Charlton (33), Robertson (33) and White (31) were already approaching retirement age as far as playing was concerned, but worryingly there was little evidence of younger talent coming through. Elwood, Foster, Lucas and McDonald were either 22 or 23 and would be a decent base unit, but only Bolland (just turning nineteen) could be considered a youngster.

The conclusion was that the squad probably had another season in them, but after that Carey was going to have to start the thankless task of changing what had been a winning side, irrespective of how Orient would fare in the First Division. Carey did manage to bring in one player, but even that was an old hand. George Waites had spent eighteen months at Norwich, but now returned to the club he had first joined in December 1958. The 24-year-old Cockney could fill in on the right wing or the right of midfield as required and his presence gave the O's more cover, rather than a stronger presence on the pitch. The fee was £5,000.

Another consideration was the fact that less than half of the squad had played First Division football and even for the old masters like Lucas, Bishop and Lea this was going to be a new experience. Whilst they had obviously played the top sides in one-off cup matches, facing the very best English football had to offer every week was going to be a considerable challenge for them. Lucas had another new experience to cope with too, because he got married in the summer. The new Mrs Lucas used to work in the club office, so she knew what being a footballer's wife was all about.

The team enjoyed a holiday in Majorca, where they embarrassingly bumped into Brian Clough, a member of the Sunderland side they had pipped for promotion, but it was in the Dutch town of Deventer that Orient geared up for their big season with a match against the local side Go-Ahead.

There was no experimentation done by Carey for this Sunday friendly on 12 August; he kept the same team that had played in the promotion-clincher with Bury; and it was his intention to start the First Division campaign with the same line-up too. He therefore probably failed to learn much from the encounter with the Dutch part-timers. Orient won the game 2-1 through goals from Graham and Dunmore in front of a healthy 12,000 crowd, but all the old O's strengths and weaknesses were apparent, namely a solid defence and a stuttering attack.

The long-awaited First Division debut for Leyton Orient was a well-chosen one. It was a home game for a start, which enabled the hard-core fans who had stayed faithful to the side in the Third Division days to enjoy their reward for all their loyalty. It was also a local derby against Arsenal, which added a zesty tang to the occasion, but just as importantly, it was an ideal test for the boys in blue.

Arsenal had spent the last three years in mid-table and had recently appointed the ex-England captain Billy Wright as boss. They had just spent £70,000 on a new player – more than Orient's entire team had cost. That man was striker Joe Baker, who remarkably was an England international who had never played in his home country before this fixture, having turned out for Hibernian and Torino. If the O's could win this one, then it would be a good omen for their chances of survival amongst the elite.

Only cup games were all-ticket at Brisbane Road, though the stands now rapidly sold out as the curious descended to watch the novelty of top-class football in London E10. A crowd of 26,300 turned out, which was still 30 short of the all-time record for a League game at Brisbane Road, set in the Third Division promotion season of 1955-56.

The whole area of Leyton seemed to have been lifted by the team's success, with a feel-good factor that boosted the whole economy as pride mingled with the extra hordes that descended on their patch. The

August sun and the big crowd did little to lift the players on the pitch, however, and disappointment ensued. Orient's defence remained as strong as ever, but there was little creativity produced near Arsenal's goal despite the Gunners' vulnerability to anyone showing flair and imagination against the soft underbelly of their defence.

The big difference between Division Two sides and top sides like Arsenal was the clinical ruthlessness that the big clubs showed in front of goal. Either side of half-time, Orient were pierced by superb individual goals by Geoff Strong and debutant Joe Baker, whilst Orient could only manage a consolation scored by Gibbs, who took advantage of confusion between the visiting keeper and his left-back. The 1-2 defeat was a warning for Orient. They didn't need to try any harder; they just had to be more clinical. The hottest thing evident at the ground this day had been a small fire in the stand that thankfully was quickly extinguished.

Carey's options for changing the team were limited by Foster's long-term injury to his calf muscle that necessitated a visit to a Harley Street specialist. He was now recovering, but White was also unavailable after a couple of niggling leg injuries. There were rumours circulating that Orient were sniffing round some of West Ham's unhappy players, and Phil Woosnam, Alan Sealey and John Bond's names were bandied about. The first two were ex-Orientals, but despite Zussman and Gore heading off to a West Ham v Wolves game, Carey denied any interest in them.

Carey persisted with his favoured eleven for the first away trip of the campaign and the result was a carbon copy of the opening match. West Brom were only a mediocre outfit like Arsenal, but that was enough. They too struck twice, this time through headers from long balls, and once more Orient's goal was a consolation, with Dunmore slipping through the offside trap to good effect. The Wednesday-night game provoked more criticism of Orient's attacking endeavours, but Carey stubbornly refused to change his team for another train journey up to England's second city three days later, when Birmingham City were the hosts.

The players used to while away those train journeys by playing cards or chatting away in little groups, whilst Les Grade was a familiar sight popping his head round the carriage doors and exchanging a cheery word with the players.

The match itself provided encouragement too, because after conceding an early goal, the visitors came back strongly through Graham and Dunmore. Poor Robertson was shamefaced about being tricked by a floated cross from Mike Hellawell that soared over his head and into the net for the equaliser, but at least the team had got a point on the board. That they had done so against a side who were likely to be struggling to stay up themselves is an indication of the difficulties that lay ahead. Many teams going up under similar circumstances enjoy a honeymoon period as the momentum and confidence from the promotion campaign carries them through the early games, but Orient enjoyed no such luck.

For the return match with West Brom, Carey maintained his commitment to the players who had won him promotion. He had vowed to keep the same line-up for the first four games and he was a man of his word. The players seemed to know that this was their last chance at a guaranteed place in the team, for they relentlessly pummelled the Albion goal in the first half, winning ten corners and pushing men forward in order to try to force a breakthrough.

Despite this domination they still trudged into the dressing-room at half-time 1-3 down, barely able to understand how it had happened. Farcical defending was the answer. Lewis had tried to clear a header from a free-kick off his own goal-line, but only succeeded in directing the ball into the roof of the net. The hapless left-back was also guilty of a fatal hesitation later on, which allowed Alec Jackson to steal in and score a goal that took an evil deflection off Lea's knee. In between these efforts, Deeley had rammed home an equaliser, but his team were unable to repeat the trick and succumbed to another soft goal when slow defending and a robust challenge by Derek Kevan against keeper Robertson gave Clive Clark an easy tap-in. Orient maintained pressure in the second half, but the deficit was too great, and all they managed was another Dunmore penalty from a magnificent charge from the lively Deeley.

September began with another derby game, this time at home to West Ham. The Hammers had been distracted by a succession of bust-ups with various players over new contracts and the disharmony within their side was evident. Bobby Moore signed a new contract just before kick-off, but this 21-year-old wing-half, who had already won five England caps, was subjected to a firestorm of intent from Orient's inspired attack.

Carey had dropped Gibbs in favour of Bolland, who was a more attacking player, and this seemed to help Dunmore from feeling quite so isolated as he had been previously. McDonald and Deeley's majestic performances on each wing were now more likely to produce a goal from the ensuing cross. Crucially, Orient managed to open the scoring for the first time in their Division One career, when Dunmore met Deeley's corner after five minutes, but Dunmore was denied a second when a long-range effort only found its way into the net via a hole in the side-netting.

As the match approached half-time, Graham received the ball inside his own half. The inside-forward had been the victim of much criticism from the home fans following their poor start to the season, but he now gave them something else to ponder. He raced into the Hammers' half, wending a path round three backtracking defenders, paused to contemplate for a split second, then ignored all the clamours for a pass and unleashed a beauty from 25 yards that screamed into the net and led to a standing ovation from even the shocked Hammers fans amongst the 24,000 crowd. West Ham were unable to fight back, not helped by an early injury to Alan Sealey, who Orient had swapped for Dunmore in March 1961.

The 2-0 win – Orient's first two-point haul of the season – lifted them out of the relegation places for a while and gave renewed heart to Carey who was about to return to his old patch. Everton had been on a surge since Carey left, with the money of John Moores and the astuteness of manager Harry Catterick combining to good effect. They had finished the previous season in fourth place, just five points behind champions Ipswich, but were now regarded as being a good bet for the title this term. Carey had bought most of their side together, so it was an interesting chance to compare past with present.

Stan Charlton recalls that Carey didn't deliver the team talk that Wednesday night, but left it to Liverpool manager Bill Shankly. The effervescent Reds boss was an ardent hater of all things Evertonian and drummed into the O's players that the Toffeemen lacked any ambition whatsoever and were ripe for the taking. The players were now inspired, but taken aback by the wall of sound that hit them as they walked out onto the pitch.

The crowd of 51,542 was the biggest by a considerable margin ever to have seen Orient play a League match, though it was still short of the 53,086 that had seen an FA Cup-tie at Aston Villa in 1929. The home fans were desperate for success, especially now that Liverpool were back in the top flight, and they went ballistic in order to avenge a shock defeat against Fulham on Saturday. For Charlton the game also recalled another match he had played at Goodison when he was with Arsenal.

He tried to clear a ball by hooking it away as he spun round, not realising that Everton's outside-left was behind him. Charlton's boot missed the ball and connected full-square with an Evertonian backside. The crowd went apoplectic at what they thought was Charlton's dirty play and referee Arthur Ellis (later to star in the TV programme *It's A Knockout*) raced over to Charlton.

Ellis put his head next to him and said: 'that were right funny. I wish I had a camera. Everybody thinks I'm telling you off, so walk away with your head down as if I had.' Ellis was generally regarded as one of the finest referees that ever blew a whistle, and this story indicates why players held him in such affection.

Another legend in black was in control today: Jack Taylor, who twelve years on was to referee the World Cup final. He blew his whistle after four minutes to signal a home goal and the crescendo of noise was unleashed once more. A Billy Bingham left-foot curler was responsible for that and he created the second with a free-kick aimed at Jimmy Gabriel's head. In between, Orient had played some pretty football, but they never looked capable of matching their more illustrious hosts. Robertson performed heroics in goal to keep the score down to reasonable proportions, but was unable to prevent a penalty from entering his net after Taylor had spotted an infringement in a goalmouth scramble. The 3-0 win lifted Everton to the top of the table, whilst Orient dropped a place to nineteenth.

O's fans were savouring every game and yet another corking home match followed on Saturday afternoon. Manchester United were the visitors, but Matt Busby had struggled to rebuild his side after the horror of the Munich air-crash four years ago and he had just signed Denis Law from Torino for a whopping £115,000, the first British transfer fee in excess of £100,000 and another example of the gulf between the top sides and the lowlier clubs.

It wasn't until 1979 that Orient got to spend that much on a player (Mervyn Day), but by then the top clubs were spending over £1 million. Despite this gap in spending ability, the old cliché is that it's still eleven against eleven and the crowd of just under 25,000 were largely unable to notice any difference in abilities on the day. Both attacks were subdued, being firmly rebuffed by a pair of keepers at the height of their abilities. Orient had created their usual modest handful of chances, aided by a midfield that was out-punching their opponents, but with the referee contemplating blowing the final whistle, it was still goalless. Then came salvation. Jeff Powell, now the *Daily Mail's* top football writer, but then tasked with covering Woodford games for the *Walthamstow Guardian*, was enjoying a day off. He recalls the magical moment when McDonald stole the ball off right-back Shay Brennan, cut inside and then floated the ball over Dave Gaskell's head and into the corner for the long-remembered winner.

Impoverished O's fans struggling to find the money to cope with all this must-see action found themselves breaking open their children's piggy-banks in order to fund another home game on the following Wednesday evening. League leaders Everton made the return trip and one can imagine that Carey sucked on his pipe a little harder as he quietly, yet determinedly told his unchanged side to go out and beat his old team.

There were 3,000 fewer spectators in the ground, though all of them were to regret missing out on this occasion. Orient's defence had kept Manchester's finest quiet, now they succeeded in shutting out the best that Everton could throw at them. They had to endure a couple of scares when Young and Vernon broke clear, but Robertson was quite literally unbeatable during that most amazing of weeks. Orient made it to half-time still on level terms, but one factor gave them an edge in attack. Everton had a couple of injuries in defence and had drafted in a couple of reserves in their place.

Orient's confident wingers and inside-forwards relished the chance to give them a roasting and this they duly did. A mighty leap and header from Lucas struck Brian Labone's body and Deeley quickly netted the rebound. Almost immediately afterwards Bolland sprayed a pass out to McDonald, who confidently beat his man and sent in a whipped low ball across the face of the goal for the hard-charging Bolland to gratefully steer in.

McDonald said afterwards that he used to be scared to try anything different because of a fear of upsetting the crowd, but now he had the confidence to go for it. The little gem then rounded off the greatest victory in Orient's history by floating over a free-kick for Dunmore to head home. The defeat pushed Everton off the top spot, whilst Orient ascended gracefully up to thirteenth. Dejected Scousers, though, had little idea that elsewhere in London the night before an event had occurred that was to make their home city famous throughout the world, for the Beatles had recorded their debut single *Love Me Do* at EMI's studios in St John's Wood.

Carey had been unable to seriously strengthen his side so far, but whether that had more to do with Zussman's firm grasp on the cheque book or an inability to find the right man is debatable. The club did manage to sign Dennis Clapton on a month's trial from Northampton, where he had only played one game since transferring from Arsenal in August 1961. The ex-England youth international was a centre-forward and was the brother of Arsenal's Danny Clapton, who was a full international and was just about to sign for Luton. In the end, nothing much came of the trial and Dennis Clapton never played another League game. It was a great pity, because the names Clapton and Orient seem to go together!

Orient had enjoyed gaining sweet revenge on Everton; now they had a chance to make amends for last season's painful FA Cup exit by beating Burnley at Turf Moor. The Clarets had narrowly missed out on the double the previous season by finishing as runners-up in both the top domestic honours, but had disappointed in the League so far. Orient were also having problems, failing to recreate the happy away days they had enjoyed in the promotion season. They valiantly defended themselves against a wave of incessant Burnley attacking, but despite another masterful example of the goalkeeping art from Robertson were unable to prevent the home side from winning 2-0. Lucas and Dunmore did their best with a pair of rasping drives each, but they couldn't make the breakthrough.

Orient enjoyed a rare midweek off, but Carey was pondering on whether to make changes for the visit of Sheffield Wednesday the following Saturday (22 September). He watched the reserves against Southend in midweek, but didn't see anyone better than the eleven he had so religiously stuck with for the majority of the season, so the lineup remained the same for the sixth successive game.

The Orient first team's routine for a home match was to enjoy a meal at their own place before relaxing. There were no strict diets to adhere to in those days, so it was up to the players to exercise commonsense in their choice of meals, though steak was a popular choice, with fish being another common item. Soon afterwards came the drive up to the ground (for the players with cars anyway), followed by a saunter down to the dressing-room to get changed. There weren't a great deal of instructions being bandied about, Carey preferred to stroll around the room telling his team to 'knock it around a bit', still with his pipe firmly wedged between his teeth. He trusted the experience of the players to be able to change the tactics off the cuff if things weren't going well, relying on his coach Baily to spit fire in the dressing room at halftime if things were still amiss.

If Carey didn't have much to say at the start of the game with Sheffield Wednesday, even the quiet, restrained boss was more than a tad worked up by the end. Wednesday's approach to the match was robust to say the least and, almost from the kick-off, Peter Swan went in hard against Dunmore. The teenage Peter Eustace followed suit and Mal Graham found himself on the wrong end of a few meaty challenges. Referee Matthews was in his first season in charge and his inexperience showed because he failed to clamp down on the players while he had the chance to do so.

This led to a gradual escalation in the severity of the tackling and players on both sides were able to get away with things that referees wouldn't normally allow, even in those days when the hard-man was king. Plenty of football was still in evidence and the goals came as fast as the fouls. Bolland and Deeley scored headers for Orient, but they were merely equalisers. As the second half wore on, the Owls managed to flick into overdrive and rattle in a couple more efforts for a convincing 4-2 win.

Poor Robertson had the kind of game every keeper dreads and he was caught either rooted to his spot or going down too slowly as the goals flowed past him. By this time, Orient were effectively down to ten men because with twenty minutes remaining Bishop was floored by a tackle from 'Bronco' Layne that left him a limping passenger for the rest of the game. Layne's tackle earned a booking (somewhat harshly, because this one didn't have the malicious intent that others had had), but it whipped up the fury of the belligerent crowd to a new height. Graham and Eustace had finally squared up to one another, though no blows were exchanged, but the final whistle saw Orient's unrulier elements race onto the pitch and surround the Wednesday players.

Whilst most of the fans contented themselves with a combination of booing and a selection of choice local expressions, one lad foolishly kicked Wednesday's skipper Peter Kay up the backside. The red-haired Kay had actually worked tirelessly to calm everyone down during the game, but even he was unable to control himself now and whipped round to deliver a swinging right hook to the ass-kicker. Layne was lucky to escape without injury too, because many O's fans were blaming him for Bishop's injury.

Fortunately for Orient they were to escape censure from the Football League because the referee had shown some wisdom by ensuring he was close to the tunnel when he blew his whistle and rapidly made his escape, thereby failing to witness the scenes at the end. He left

Brisbane Road with a police escort and the cops were also deployed around the visiting team coach to protect the Wednesday players.

Three of those Wednesday players (Kay, Layne and Swan) would be sentenced in 1965 to a brief spell at Her Majesty's Pleasure and banned from football for conspiring to fix a defeat against Ipswich in December 1962 in order to win a bet. Two other lower-division matches were rigged that day and rumours abounded about many others over the years, though no one will ever know the full extent of match-rigging at the time.

Orient were keen to raise money by more legitimate means and they announced a Development Scheme Draw to be run by ex-player Johnny Hartburn. The hope was that agents on commission would flog tickets at a cost to the punter of a shilling a week and that a prize fund would be established that might net the lucky winner as much as £100 a week. If the scheme reached its potential it would raise as much as £750 a week for the club, with the Supporters Club doing the majority of the work, maintaining a fine tradition of helping to fund the club that they love so much.

The supporters must have still thought it strange that their League Cup second round tie at Newcastle was against lower division opposition, but the Toon were just outside the Second Division promotion places. Carey may have been ultra-conservative in his team selections for League matches, but he was forced to use this game as a chance to experiment with a different line-up. Three changes were forced upon him: Bishop was going to be out for a few weeks with his sprained ankle, and David Clark was drafted in to make his second first-team appearance.

Keeper Robertson and left-back Lewis were also victims of Sheffield Wednesday's over-enthusiastic tackling and Frank George came back into the green jersey for the first time since February, whilst the replacement for Lewis was Bill Taylor. Mal Graham was the only tactical omission, physical and mental tiredness playing a part, so George Waites was able to make his first O's start since his re-signing at the start of the season. His previous appearance for the first team had come on New Year's Eve 1960.

The Geordies retained some fondness for the new competition and the 22,490 attendance was the highest of the night. Most of them spent much of the game disappointed though, because Orient did play like a team from a higher level, at least until the ball reached the forwards. Both keepers could have stayed in the dressing room for the first half and still kept a clean sheet, such was the 'quality' of the shooting, but Bolland showed everyone where the net was soon after the restart with a header from Deeley's corner.

The corner-taker had a goal disallowed soon afterwards, but Orient were all set for a sneaky 1-0 win when disaster struck twice. Firstly Robertson had to be helped off after 73 minutes, forcing Charlton into the goal as his rough-and-ready replacement. He kept the Geordies at bay for thirteen minutes, but flapped at a header from Ken Hale, forcing Lucas to demonstrate his keeping skills with a clearing punch. The referee wasn't impressed and awarded a penalty, but Lucas wasn't even booked, let alone sent off. Jimmy Fell converted the kick and Orient went away unhappy.

Well, perhaps not all of Orient were miserable at the draw. Was Zussman secretly suppressing a grin at the thought of a bit more gate money coming their way in a replay? His club were still short of cash and this was illustrated to Charlton once when he went in to ask for a wage rise. He was on £43 10s a week at the time, but Carey went and showed the player the club's account book which demonstrated that there was no more cash in the pot. Charlton went away contented, despite not being able to wring any more money from the boss.

Whilst Les Gore was busy dealing with the queue for treatment outside his trainer's surgery, Eddie Baily concentrated on the light training regime needed when the team was playing twice a week. There was plenty of variety in the schedule and a real sense of camaraderie within the squad that was certainly apparent to the players with experience at other clubs, where cliques were much more in evidence.

Gore had patched up all bar Bishop from the Wednesday mauling and Graham was back in favour, so it was the familiar line-up that greeted the travelling contingent in the 26,505 crowd on Saturday, 29 September at Fulham, apart from Clark at No 5. With comedian Tommy Trinder an established part of the Craven Cottage set-up, there was a similar show-business backdrop to the game that Orient enjoyed with Delfont and Grade. The Fulham players were definitely of the amateur dramatics society standard though, and Orient really had to beat them if they were going to stay up this season. Johnny Haynes may have been on £100 a week, but he was injured and no good to them. Judging by the way his team were struggling, they barely deserved that amount between them.

Even the return of Bobby Robson to their line-up after a six-year interregnum at West Brom hadn't changed their reputation of being relegation strugglers; and so it proved. Orient were able to cruise to their first away win of the season without much effort, with a couple of goals before half-time. The reporter from *The Times* summed up Orient's performance succinctly: 'They are no more than a competent side but they play within their limitations.'

That win hoisted the O's up to twelfth in the table, the highest position that they have ever achieved in their history. O's fans could study the statistics and bask in an aura of reflected pride. They were above the mighty Manchester United, champions Ipswich, and London rivals West Ham, Arsenal and Fulham.

	P	Pts
1 Wolves	11	19
2 Everton	11	17
3 Tottenham	11	15
4 Burnley	11	15
5 Leicester	11	14
6 Sheff Wed	11	14
7 Nott'm For	11	14
8 Sheff Utd	11	13
9 Aston Villa	11	13
10 West Brom	11	12
11 Liverpool	11	9
12 ORIENT	11	9

There was no rest for the players, because Monday evening saw the League Cup replay take place at Brisbane Road. Zussman's hopes for a bumper gate were dashed by a lowly crowd of 8,037, many being put off at the thought of being drowned in a torrential downpour. They missed a corker of a game. Lucas embarrassed himself after five minutes by steering a sliding attempted clearance past his own keeper, but twenty minutes later Orient were ahead. Dunmore and Deeley danced down the wings and delivered delightful crosses for Bolland and Graham to head in. Alan Suddick popped up with an equaliser to make it 2-2 and for the first time at Brisbane Road a first-class match went into extra-time.

Not long after the restart the Orient floodlights (which were only two years old) suddenly went out. The players passed the ball amongst themselves, lit up by the stand lights, which stayed on. Many spectators were perhaps waiting for the sight of Zussman running along to stick another shilling in the meter, but it was a faulty switch that caused the blackout.

Good though the games had been, both sides would have dreaded the thought of having to do this all over again, especially Newcastle, with the long trek they had suffered. Thankfully power was restored seven minutes later and, just to make sure there would be no rematch, Orient wrapped the game up with a couple of goals in a two-minute spell near the end, scored by Graham and Deeley. Though Dunmore hadn't found his way onto the scoresheet, he had created three of the goals and impressed the Geordie legend Jackie Milburn who stated: 'If there's a better centre-forward than Dave Dunmore in the League today – show him to me.'

Rumours abounded that Orient were interested in signing one Newcastle old-boy, Arsenal's George Eastham. Given that Arsenal had spent £47,500 on the inside-forward just two years before, there was no chance that the O's could seriously have contemplated buying him, though Carey did say with a twinkle in his eye that they could maybe stretch to £6,000. In the event, Eastham stayed with the Gunners until 1966 before becoming a legend at Stoke.

After beating one relegation-threatened side away from home, Orient were hopeful of doing the double by dispatching Manchester City, who were in a similar position. They certainly dominated the possession, but reverted back to type by failing to convert any chances, though Dunmore was unlucky when his long-distance shot banged the crossbar. Graham was especially profligate, wasting three good efforts, but the home side were ruthless, sticking away the only two chances that fell their way.

Two days later, on Monday, 8 October, Orient hosted a friendly match against the Dutch side ADO. Orient had a large Jewish following and as the match coincided with the Holy Day of 'Yom Kippur', the match didn't kick-off till 8.30pm to enable them to get to the ground after the synagogues closed at 8 o'clock.

Carey resisted the chance to make wholesale changes, merely resting Bolland and McDonald and bringing in Foster and Elwood. The manager was very conservative with his team selection even when things were going badly, but even so, most bosses would surely have rested their key players for a meaningless match in the middle of the season. Perhaps he was trying to get his team to pile up a few confidence-building goals against inferior opposition, but if so he was only partly successful. Dunmore did manage to break his personal barren spell with a couple of shots, but for 58 minutes they had bombarded the Dutch goal with no success whatsoever.

The visitors did pull a goal back with a late penalty, generously gifted to them by Lea's stray arm which connected with the ball in the penalty area, and the match ended 2-1 to the O's. Carey probably learnt nothing from the exercise, but Luton's chief scout George Martin did get a look at Foster, though nothing became of it. Speculation about the out-of-favour player was growing, with Brighton and Plymouth also apparently registering an interest, but for the time being he remained an Oriental.

The O's took their Dutch friends on a shopping and sightseeing trip the next day, followed by dinner, but Les Gore was still busy mending the crocks. Bishop, George and White were coming along nicely, but reserve centre-forward Mike Hollow had broken a bone in his foot and was out for a month. He had to wait until the following season to get into the first team. Carey did finally make a new signing, but not before offloading Ron Newman for £5,000 to Crystal Palace, where the neglected winger hoped to experience first-team football once more. The new man coming in was a goalkeeper – Mike Pinner.

Pinner was born in Boston in February 1934 and was a goalkeeper in his school team. He went to Cambridge University in 1952 and also spent time at England's new coaching establishment at Lilleshall, working out with professional coaches. Eventually he joined the joint Oxford and Cambridge University side called Pegasus and he played in goal for them, on and off, as a guest over the next ten years. Aston Villa's manager, Eric Houghton, knew Pinner because they both hailed from Boston and after a spell in the youth team he graduated into the first team, playing four times for them from the 1954-55 season onwards. He left university and started training as a solicitor, vowing only to play for clubs that would accept this. Because of this, Pinner didn't sign professional terms and remained an amateur.

Pinner left Villa in 1957 and became something of a nomad, turning out for teams who needed urgent goalkeeping cover. He played once for the famous amateur side Corinthian Casuals, before enjoying a seven-game spell with Sheffield Wednesday over the course of two seasons. He then moved down to London to continue his work as a solicitor and in 1959 joined QPR, playing nineteen League games for them. He had a four-game spell at Manchester United and also had an odd game with Chelsea and Swansea. He became first-choice keeper in England's amateur side and became the only player to win as many as

50 amateur caps in the post-war period, eventually earning 52. He played in the 1956 and 1960 Olympic Games and came across many top-class players over the years, including a young Franz Beckenbauer.

Pinner used many club's training grounds to keep himself fit and was a familiar sight at Orient, because he lived only twenty minutes away. He used to train with the youngsters on Tuesday and Thursday nights and naturally enough was well-placed when Carey decided he needed an extra pair of hands in the Orient net.

Robertson retained his place in goal for the home game against Blackpool on Saturday, 13 October. Waites was the returning prodigal son and he took the No 8 shirt off Bolland. The new old-boy had a chance to score in the opening minute but Tony Waiters made a good save.

Orient kept plugging away with their short-passing game, but once more the inside-forwards were heavily criticised for not holding the ball up and creating opportunities for the strikers. Blackpool used a more direct approach and plundered the two goals they needed through Ray Parry, who was quick to punish rare mistakes in Orient's defence. The most memorable aspect of the day, which enthralled most of the 17,156 spectators present, was the spectacle of left-winger McDonald trying to get the better of England international right-back Jimmy Armfield.

McDonald worked his way through his full repertoire of tricks, but time and time again Armfield casually took the ball off him. The O's fans found themselves in the situation of bystanders about to watch an impending road traffic accident, not wanting to watch but unable to take their eyes off the painful end result. The 0-2 defeat also had another effect which made grim viewing for O's fans. It pushed their team down five places in the table to nineteenth – just four off the bottom.

A home match against struggling Fourth Division side Chester in the League Cup third round on Wednesday evening gave everyone a welcome break from the gathering gloom surrounding Orient's League prospects. Carey rang the changes, though mostly they were enforced: Taylor replaced Lewis at left-back, Bishop made a welcome return in the half-back line, and a new face appeared wearing the No 11 shirt, normally the preserve of McDonald who was injured. Roger Wedge had 90 minutes in which to impress the cautious Carey.

Wedge had a mediocre game and disappointingly was the only forward player not to score a goal. After a quiet opening spell of 38 minutes in which only Waites had found the net, Orient finally realised that they were in a completely different class to their opponents and react-ed accordingly. For the remainder of the match Chester's goal took on the appearance of a coconut shy as virtually the whole team queued up to have a pot shot at keeper John Hardie, who became a coconut for the night. The poor keeper stooped down nine times to pick the ball out of his net, whilst Robertson at the other end did so twice near the end as Orient tired of the game, in much the same way as a cat tires of tormenting a mouse.

You might think that a 9-2 victory (still a record cup win for the club) would be greeted with euphoria, but in those days it wasn't unusu-al for the top clubs to thrash lower-division sides and the reports were not as sensationalist as they would be today. This is a bit harsh on Waites and Graham, who both helped themselves to a hat-trick, though there is no record of whether they fought to retain the match ball at the end.

Poor Wedge never got another chance to play in the Orient first team and, for the trip up to Aston Villa in Division One, Deeley switched wings to play on the left, whilst Waites showed his versatility by playing on the right. Bolland came back into the side, but the differ-ence in class between Chester and Villa was vast and once more the for-wards fired blanks against a top-drawer defence. Loyal visiting sup-porters would claim that their side would have picked up a point if the referee had spotted a blatant handball from Charlie Aitken, but the truth is that Villa deserved the 1-0 victory, especially considering the fact that over half their side was made up of reserves. The reason for this was the Home International Championship.

Younger readers might not realise that throughout the course of the season, England, Scotland, Wales and Northern Ireland would play each other, and the side at the top of the mini-league at the end would be declared Home International Champions. Mal Lucas proudly donned the red shirt of Wales for a home match against holders Scotland the same day, although his side lost 2-3 as Scotland went on to retain their championship. Lucas did quite well, but the Welsh side were obviously a collection of individuals against the more united Scotsmen. Star players for the Welsh were John Charles (Leeds), Ivor Allchurch (Cardiff) and Cliff Jones (Spurs), whilst Scotland featured Pat Crerand (Celtic), Ian St John (Liverpool) and Denis Law (Manch-ester United).

Non-travelling O's fans weren't forgotten, because on the same day the Football Combination Championship (1961-62) took place at

Leyton Stadium, the formal name for Brisbane Road. Orient had won the midweek section of the competition last season and Spurs the Saturday version. Over 9,000 fans witnessed the encounter, boosted by the fact that the Spurs and West Ham games were postponed because of the Home International Championship, but a very strong Spurs outfit just shaded it 1-0. The quality of the opposition can be gauged by the fact that the winning goal was created by Terry Dyson and Frank Saul and scored by Bobby Smith. All three were regulars in Tottenham's first team. Orient did well to outplay Spurs for much of the match, but fired blanks in familiar fashion. The O's team was: Pinner, Russell, Deeks, Payne J, Clark, Gregory, White, Foster, Wedge, Elwood, McDonald.

CHAPTER SIX

Snowed Under

(October 1962 – March 1963)

Orient manager John Carey pronounced his opinions on things Orient, now that they had made it through a third of the season. 'Our main hope is to try to restore the confidence we had five or six weeks ago. Last season everybody played just a little bit above themselves to lift us up into the First Division. They did the same when we beat Everton and Manchester United this season. Now something has gone completely haywire. Against Villa on Saturday we had no cohesion and no fight. But we had two long sessions this week working on it and I feel we may come up with something – like beating Spurs tomorrow. We are always interested in players, but we would have to pay £25,000 to £30,000 for the right man and then we can't be sure we will get what we want.'

Most pundits reckoned that Orient desperately needed an inside-forward who could become a strong link-man from the half-back line to the forwards, or a striker who could relieve some of the burden on the overworked Dunmore. The possibility of Dunmore getting injured and the consequences for the team didn't bear thinking about for anyone with Orient's interests at heart.

Another one of the myriad of names linked with a possible move to Orient was Arsenal's John Barnwell, who was stuck in their reserves, but even he would have been far too expensive at £25,000, even if either the club or the player had shown any inclination for a move, which they hadn't.

Orient did have the possibility of even more goalkeeping cover because Dave Groombridge stated a desire to return to his old club. Groombridge had been Orient's second-choice keeper for almost the entire 1950s, but two years ago had undergone extensive reconstructive surgery on his left knee. Sadly he was never destined to turn out for the first team ever again.

As Carey mentioned, Orient were pitched against Tottenham Hotspur in the season's most eagerly awaited fixture at Brisbane Road, on Saturday, 27 October. Although Tottenham had relinquished their League title to rank outsiders Ipswich Town the season before, the FA Cup holders were still generally regarded as the most powerful team in the country.

With the two clubs being less than five miles apart, it was easy for visiting supporters to descend *en masse* on Leyton and the attendance for the game was recorded as 30,987 – a complete sell-out. The previous record for a League game at Brisbane Road (26,330 v Torquay in 1956) was smashed, though the current record is 33,363 against Birmingham City in 1972). It should be remembered that a previous Orient v Spurs game at the old Millfields Road ground attracted 37,615 in 1929.

To mark the occasion, Orient made a bit of extra effort with the programme, putting in a special centre-spread with facsimiles of both team's autographs. It must be said that Orient's programme wasn't particularly good, even by the lowly standards of the day. Typically, the home programme for this season would consist of twenty pages and the page size was even smaller than A5, though even that was far bigger than the previous season's effort.

The cover featured the victorious team from last season, with a blue hue to it, and the opponents and date and time of kick-off, together with the price of sixpence (2½p). After a full page advert for Senior Service cigarettes, there was a page with the club's main details and personnel, listing the official ground name as Leyton Stadium, Brisbane Road, E10. The telephone number at the time was Leytonstone 1368. There were nearly two pages of 'Oriental Chatter' by 'Forester', with details of upcoming games featuring Orient in Division One, the Football Combination and the Seanglian League.

Both teams line-ups were listed on page six, with the other games taking place in the First Division being given a letter alongside them. This was so that boards could be displayed alongside the advertising hoardings, with the half-time scores of each game shown next to the corresponding letter. Pen pictures of the opposition would follow, with several adverts either side of the usual centre-spread of an action photograph. League tables would be shown and Orient's fixture list gained a page of its own.

A couple more pages of pictures were featured, before a page of Supporters Club Notes by their Chairman FW Dunn. An advert for British Railways regularly appeared on the back page, often with prices for the next away destination. For the Tottenham fixture, and for every home game till the end of the season, Orient did something to encourage further programme sales. If you were lucky enough to find a programme with the initials of George Hicks (there was one per issue) you would be given a ticket for the FA Cup final – the hottest ticket in town, no matter what Les Grade and Bernard Delfont might think.

The banter between rival fans flowed freely on the way to the game, especially as many Spurs fans resided in the Leyton area. At last Orient's dedicated fans, both young and old, were able to walk with heads high as bragging rights were fought for, at least before the game! The home fans noted that Mike Pinner was making his debut in goal, ahead of Robertson.

Pinner had the appearance of an archetypal mad professor with a bald patch in the middle of his head and tufts of black hair either side, though his playing style was far more flamboyant than either Robertson or George. He preferred to stay close to the edge of the penalty area, encouraging the defenders to push up to the halfway line. Although he was described by one scribe as being 'as quick as a panther', he was not universally acclaimed, with some openly doubting whether this 'gifted amateur' could attain the standards of professional keepers. His quick reactions led him to hold back often and watch what was happening and then react to it, rather than anticipating and being more pre-emptive in his movements. Some called him a 'Flash Harry'.

Pinner adjudged himself to be happy with his debut, even though he conceded five goals. White put Spurs in front after 21 minutes, but five minutes later the recalled Foster craftily slipped a fine ball through to Deeley, who prompted an enormous roar by slamming the ball into the back of the net. Orient remained on level terms for nearly ten minutes, but then Tottenham's extra bit of class really started to emerge. Pinner was unlucky with a Tony Marchi shot that deflected wildly off the shoulder of Bishop, and Spurs added further goals through Terry Medwin, John White and Cliff Jones.

Though long-standing O's fans would have to go back to 1950 to recall a heavier home defeat (2-7 v Aldershot), it was far from the thrashing that it at first appears. Orient played well, with Tottenham's defence being given a good testing, but the home team were just unable to cope with the side who they had so assiduously modelled themselves on.

Also, Orient were not the only team to wilt under a Spurs onslaught. Already this season, the new League leaders had destroyed the likes of Ipswich (5-1 away), West Ham (6-1 away), Nottingham Forest (9-2) and

Manchester United (6-2). Carey was satisfied, declaring that 'the lads showed a lot more spirit and determination altogether'. Unfortunately, no points are awarded for these fine qualities, and Orient were dumped onto the foot of the table as a result.

	P	Pts
18 Liverpool	14	11
19 Ipswich	15	10
20 Manchester U	15	10
21 Fulham	15	10
22 ORIENT	15	9

Orient entered November with a desire to forget about the four League defeats suffered during October. The injury to Bishop was regarded by Carey as being the turning point of the season, but now that he was available, they had to try and bounce back against a Nottingham Forest side which was lying seventh in the table, despite that recent pummelling by Spurs.

The main reason for their success was down to winning all their previous six games at the City Ground, but they met their match against a focused O's side. Though Forest took the lead, when Pinner went AWOL at a critical time, an equaliser was forthcoming through Dunmore, ending his personal drought of seven goalless League games. The visitors should have gone on to win, but once more their failure to snap up half-chances cost them dearly.

Carey was unable to track down any inside-forwards at the right price, so he promoted a teenager from the reserves instead. Harry Gregory was a gangly teenager, similar to Bolland, whose place he took. The ex-Hackney schoolboy had cracked in seven goals for the reserves, earning a positional change from the wing-half's role to inside-forward. He had also turned out for the England Youth team. Carey's ditched his conservative instincts in playing him, stating that 'this boy has proved he can get the goals consistently. He's got the height and is a fine prospect.'

League champions Ipswich were the visitors to Brisbane Road for his Gregory's debut, and Orient had the honour of being able to switch places with the spectacularly under-performing Suffolk side if they could win. The cause of their demise was largely down to the fact that their tactic of linking deep-lying wingers with two giant front men had been well and truly sussed out.

Carey's pre-match pronouncements on Gregory were apt, as he took only fourteen minutes to find the net. He tired quickly though, and had substitutes been in place at that time, then no doubt he would have been replaced before the end. Ipswich hit back with two goals in quick succession and the game was up, despite Dunmore having the chance to level from the penalty spot as Andy Nelson illegally felled him in the area.

Dunmore was usually a dead-eye from twelve yards, but today he sent his kick just a little bit too close to the keeper and Roy Bailey was able to deflect it downwards onto the line and pounce quickly onto it. Even the deadpan expression of Ipswich manager Alf Ramsey was spotted breaking into a grin as his side successfully held on to both points.

Two days later, on Monday, 12 November, came a fourth round League Cup clash at home to Charlton, which attracted fewer than 10,000. George and Lucas returned to the side, pushing Pinner and Lea out of the team.

The visitors were Second Division opponents on paper, but matched Orient in all but scoring. Orient led 3-2 after only 33 minutes, with Foster rising high to head in two corners either side of yet another poach from the new boy Gregory. The Haddicks went manic in the second half, peppering the charmed home goal with shots, yet failing to score, usually Orient's failing. With Fulham succumbing 0-1 at Norwich, Leyton Orient was now London's sole representative, though it must be mentioned that Arsenal and Spurs had chosen not to enter the competition.

A visit to Anfield followed, but there was to be no repeat of last season's heroics as Liverpool hit five goals without reply. The main architect of the defeat was Roger Hunt who earned himself the right to keep the match ball with a hat-trick, but Ian St John and Billy Stevenson also netted. George was making his First Division debut for the O's, but like Pinner he had a great game whilst still contriving to concede five. As reports of the game filtered back to London, O's fans must have been convinced that it would take a remarkable change to save their status now.

Carey now abandoned all his instincts for making subtle team-changes, if at all, and thoroughly confused the home fans by playing Dunmore as a right-winger, Lucas as an outside-left, and Taylor and Gregory as strikers for the game against Wolves. At least Lewis and Gibbs returned to their usual defensive roles. Orient had missed the formidable presence of Lewis especially. Extremely slow and bulky for a left-back, the defender showed all the manoeuvrability of a juggernaut in a cul-de-sac, but made up for this by using that otherwise wasted time in order to think about what he was doing. Stan Charlton recalls one game in which Lewis was openly debating which leg he should use to tackle an opposing right-winger, bemusing his colleague who used to tackle instinctively without giving it much consideration.

It took addled O's fans virtually all the game to figure out who was playing where, and it seems as though the players were having similar problems because Wolves racked up four goals without reply, despite the pitch, which had reverted to its usual late autumn consistency of thick cloying mud with just a smattering of grass as an afterthought. Despite it's unattractiveness as a playing surface, opposition manager Stan Cullis declared that he would like to wrap it up and take it home with him, though no doubt he would rather have had the O's team as opposition every week.

With time rapidly running out to turn things around, Carey continued to make drastic changes. He offloaded Foster to Grimsby for £10,000, reckoning that the inside-forward wasn't his old self after his earlier injury. Foster later joined Reading, Dallas (USA), Brentford and Ramsgate before going full-time into the cabinet-making business. He was still doing that when he died.

Waites was sold to Brighton for less than that, though Orient recouped all the money they had spent on him in the summer. He later joined Millwall (but didn't play for the first team) before turning out for Gravesend & Northfleet. He became a greengrocer in Watford and his son Paul was on the books of his local club. His heart was still in Leyton though, and when he died in August 2000 he insisted that all the flowers were in red and white – Orient's colours.

Elwood was another reserve who was keen to move, but he remained for the time being. This extra cash, combined with pressure being placed on the board for more money, gave Carey a rumoured £40,000 transfer kitty to play with. Carey's first target was Tottenham's out-of-favour left-back Mel Hopkins, who was valued at £17,000. The intention was to play Hopkins in his favourite position and move the giant figure of Lewis forward where he could terrify the opposition defenders. All this theory was in vain though, because the green light changed to red as everyone failed to agree terms.

A visit to Blackburn was scheduled for the first day of December 1962 and Carey abandoned his reckless team changes and reverted to a familiar line-up, with all the players back in their favourite positions. Pinner returned to the first team, whilst McDonald was a welcome sight back on the left wing with Graham alongside him. George, Gibbs and Taylor were the players who were axed to make way for them.

Carey used his inside knowledge of his old team to mark Bryan Douglas out of the game, but even so Pinner would have been justified in putting in a claim for overtime as he explored every inch of mud in his goalmouth at close quarters with a succession of spectacular saves. He nearly got decapitated by the equaliser as hot-shot Mike Harrison (from Ilford) let rip from ten yards, but Orient were grateful for the point.

Monday saw another League Cup night at Brisbane Road, but the meagre crowd of 6,000 obviously implies that not many saw Orient as potential winners of the trophy, though the thick fog and bitter cold did little to attract a large crowd. Bury may have been Second Division material, but they were looking to 'do an Orient', as they were lying in second place in the table.

The absent home fans were better off with their cup of Horlicks in front of an open fire, because Bury earned themselves a place in the two-legged semi-final against Birmingham without much effort at all. An early goal helped them on their way, with the home defence looking as if the fog had robbed them of any sense of where each other were positioned. The absence of injured players Lucas and Graham didn't help and Gibbs and Taylor were largely anonymous. Another goal just before time confirmed the inevitable and it was a chastened team who left the next day for a week's 'toning-up' at the chilly resort of Broadstairs.

A home match with Sheffield United in the League did nothing to restore the crowds and under 10,000 made it through the turnstiles. This time the absentees were punished by missing one of the most spectacular goals seen at Brisbane Road for a long time. Graham collected the ball from well inside his own half, before accelerating past three less-than-sharp Blades and cracking home the sweetest of right-foot shots. A dodgy looking penalty decision led to the equaliser, with Lea protesting his innocence as Keith Kettleborough tumbled under his challenge, but despite falling behind midway through the second half, Orient bounced back to earn their second successive point with a Dunmore header.

Orient had graciously accepted an invitation to play a friendly at Walthamstow Avenue to mark the Isthmian League club's inauguration of their £5,000 floodlights at Green Pond Road. Carey put out a strong team, using seven of the players from the previous game, but giving George, Clark, Gregory and Elwood the chance to put forward a case for inclusion into the first team. They didn't take it. The home side were determined to embarrass their more illustrious neighbours and this they duly did by winning the game 3-0. As if that wasn't bad enough, Dunmore limped off before the end with a leg injury and the lights dimmed once more on the O's.

Carey was by now getting desperate to strengthen his team and he joined a mini-auction bidding for the services of West Ham's prolific outside-left Malcolm Musgrove. Fellow-strugglers Fulham were also keen to catch the player with a rumoured £11,000 price tag, though he received a wild-card offer from Peterborough United to become their player-manager.

Whilst those negotiations continued, further names were linked with the O's on a weekly basis, or so it seemed. Charlton's Stuart Leary and Newcastle's Barrie Thomas were named, but the proposed Thomas deal was for a player swap with Dunmore which Carey didn't want. He would have considered an offer for Thomas to play alongside Dunmore, but not replace him. Another player-exchange rumour featured Mal Lucas and Arsenal's Gerry Ward, but both clubs denied that speculation. One problem that Carey was having was persuading ambitious players to join them. It was a *Catch-22* situation. Orient wouldn't stay up without fresh blood, but most players didn't want to join a club that looked doomed to relegation.

The season now entered its second half and Orient's 22nd League fixture involved a short journey to north London to visit Highbury. Arsenal were a comparatively unattractive team at this time, certainly when compared to their great rivals Tottenham, and this, combined with the effects of Christmas being only ten days away and the subsequent exodus to the shops, inevitably drained the crowd level to under 30,000.

With Dunmore still injured, Bolland was given the difficult job of replacing him. Gregory took the place of Taylor and therefore it was an unusually youthful-looking side that was faced with the task of outgunning the Gunners, with Joe Baker as chief sniper. The Arsenal striker took only eleven minutes to add his name to the scoresheet and took the same amount of time in the second half to repeat the feat. Pinner was to blame for both goals. He preferred not to come out for crosses, but to leave it for his defenders to deal with if possible. On these two occasions he hesitated, which allowed Baker to snaffle up the half-chances to ensure a 2-0 victory. Not that Pinner was solely to blame for the defeat. He redeemed himself to some extent with a collection of fine stops and had the Orient wingers come up trumps against Arsenal's inexperienced wingmen, then the outcome might have been more favourable.

Malcolm Musgrove decided to throw his lot in with Leyton Orient and Carey immediately thrust him into the home game against Birmingham City, with McDonald making way for him. Lucas was back at No 4, so Gibbs moved forward and replaced Gregory. O's fans burned their eyes on their new £11,000 man and they didn't have to wait long to see what he could do. Racing in from the left, his first shot as an Orient player was a goal.

Bolland too was a rare visitor to the goalscoring charts and his contribution was a satisfying volley from a back-header by Graham. Orient were well on top and creating enough good chances to run up a hefty score, but they were all squandered. Birmingham were patient and gradually wore down the home side in the second half. Jimmy Bloomfield took his chances and levelled the scores, but in the last minute there was controversy.

A howl of protest erupted around the end where City's Colin Green appeared to punch a goal-bound shot away. The referee consulted his linesman and waved away the home team's protests. Such is life, but at least the O's were starting to pick up the odd point now and again. Unfortunately many clubs around them had started to win matches, so the two smaller London clubs were looking isolated. Incidentally, the football schedule had been wrecked by fog, with Fulham's home game called off and seven League matches abandoned, including that at Watford.

	P	Pts
18 Ipswich	23	18
19 Manchester C	22	18
20 Blackpool	22	18
21 Fulham	22	15
22 ORIENT	23	13

Dunmore's return to the forward line was a welcome Boxing Day present for disheartened O's fans looking at the League table. Bolland was trying to aid and abet him, with Gibbs winning back the No 4 shirt off Lucas who had fractured his fibula – in other words broken his leg. He was due to be out for six weeks.

Leicester was the destination for the tiny handful of Orient fans who managed to see their team play, and they saw Stan Charlton being credited with the opening goal after four minutes. It was a great pity that it was an own-goal and that a fellow defender Frank McLintock was the one who inflicted his pain.

Leicester were the season's surprise challengers for the title and they ended the day third in the table after plucking Orient's defence clean and then stuffing them. Orient were four goals down at the break and were denied the usual comforting words from manager Carey, who was in Scotland. Instead, coach Eddie Baily gave them the benefit of his opinions in a forthright manner and his harsh words helped staunch the flow of goals against, indeed they even managed to add a late consolation through Musgrove to keep the score down to 1-5.

The reason Carey was over the border was his endless quest for new talent. The object of his interest was Willie Penman, who Rangers had placed on the transfer list. He certainly impressed Carey, netting a hat-trick in a 6-1 win over St Mirren reserves, but manager Scott Symon didn't want to part with Penman until after the New Year because of their heavy fixture list, and he was also looking for a player-exchange, instead of cash.

There was nobody at Orient who interested the Rangers boss though, and Carey went away empty-handed. Penman eventually signed for Newcastle. Carey also had an eye on their left-back, but his talent-spotting antics were curtailed by the worsening weather situation and he rushed back to London whilst he could.

Dunmore's name was forever being linked with other clubs, especially with Brian Clough injured at Sunderland, and Eddie Baily was offered the opportunity to apply for the vacant manager's job at Reading which he graciously declined.

Orient were scheduled to play the return match against Leicester City on 29 December, but the day before the Brisbane Road pitch lay under four inches of snow. World Cup referee Ken Aston inspected the surface and declared it unable to yield to a stud and promptly postponed the match.

Surprisingly, within a good kick of the ground, Leyton Youths' game went ahead, with their League's general secretary declaring that the ground was soft underneath and that it was quite safe and fun. Obviously spoken by someone who didn't have to play that day!

The winter of 1962-63 has gone down in folklore as probably the worst since 1946-47. A combination of heavy snow and biting cold kept the temperature below freezing for weeks at a time. The snow came down heavily in London over the New Year and soon Walthamstow Council had switched almost every worker from every department into snow-clearing duties, concentrating on keeping the main roads clear.

Brisbane Road was meant to be the venue for the FA Cup third round tie against Hull on 5 January, and in desperation Orient used heavy machinery and snowploughs to dump 150 tons of snow onto the terraces, but there was never going to be the slightest chance of the game going ahead, because there was no way of getting rid of that 150 tons of snow from the ground. The club did manage to clear a double-file running track for the players to exercise on, but nobody was keen on staying outside for long, and most fitness work was done under cover where possible.

Mal Lucas received little sympathy from some teasing colleagues who speculated that his broken leg was a deliberate ploy to stay in the warm for the winter. Although Orient had a medical officer, a Dr Bell, Lucas preferred to go and see West Ham's physio Bill Jenkins for advice, either at Upton Park or at the Jenkins' abode. His advice was to liaise with Les Gore and then get an X-ray at Whipps Cross Hospital. They located the fracture, but Jenkins told the medics not to put the leg in plaster because he wanted to work on the leg, to stop the muscle from wasting away. The ill wind that kept the unfavourable weather systems over Britain for so long did blow some good for the crocked Welshman, who used the time to recover.

The FA Cup-tie with Hull was scheduled four times in the next three weeks and postponed each time. Eventually it suffered ten postponements, which was much less than some ties. The match between Coventry and Lincoln was called off fifteen times. Just three of the 32 ties were played as originally scheduled (at Plymouth, Preston and Tranmere) and one of them ended in a draw, so the traditional draw for the fourth round on the Monday featured 62 teams, with only Sunderland and West Brom definitely through. 'Leyton Orient or Hull City will play Derby County or Peterborough United' didn't help anybody plan anything much.

Even at this early stage though, the Football League approached the FA with a view to extending the League season by an extra two Saturdays to accommodate the 135 postponed League games so far.

This was nodded through, because by then the thaw had started and everything was expected to return to normal shortly, as all the main roads and railways were clear in the South.

The thaw did not last. The raw easterly wind froze most of the country once more, and on 12 January only five professional League and Cup matches took place in the whole of England and Wales, although unusually Scotland fared slightly better. The West Ham versus Orient game was an early casualty. Whilst Brisbane Road only had 1½ inches of ice on the pitch – thanks to the earlier snow-clearing efforts – Upton Park had five inches, a deliberate ploy to try to insulate the grass underneath. Both Dagenham and Walthamstow played home games this day on heavily sanded pitches, but their actions were criticised for risking injury to the players. One of the objections came from Leytonstone, who wanted their FA Amateur Cup-tie at Dagenham postponed. The game went ahead, but it was Leytonstone who won the match!

Everyone connected with football was now getting thoroughly fed up. Carey couldn't judge players unless it was by skating ability, players were more concerned with keeping warm than keeping fit and the fans were stuck inside the house on Saturdays, with road and rail links liable to be out of action at any time. The players themselves were now spending their days mostly under one of the stands, doing whatever they could to keep fit, including running up and down stairwells.

Saturday, 19 January should have been an exciting day in Orient's season with a visit to Old Trafford, but only games at Villa, Spurs and Wolves went ahead in Division One. Charlton also attempted a home game in Division Two and their experience illustrates the difficulties faced by the clubs during this exceptional time. First of all there was a power cut which delayed the kick-off.

This was a frequent experience as electrical systems failed under the intense cold, not helped by an overtime ban imposed by the unions on the workers who would have been required to repair them. Burst water mains were another major problem at the time, but Charlton seemed to have avoided that curse on this day. The Valley still had a considerable layer of snow and ice on it, but it was heavily sanded in places. All the lines on the pitch had been marked out in blue and a traditional orange ball was used.

The players did their best, but they were having immense difficulties staying upright on the ice. Once they fell over there was a real danger of serious injury as the ground was as hard as concrete. The weather ended this farce, a blizzard swept in ten minutes into the second half and the referee had no choice but to call it a day, probably to the relief of the long-suffering supporters who were in danger of the effects of hypothermia.

And so it went on. Although there wasn't as much snow as there had been in previous extreme winters, and several days had notable periods of sunshine, the temperature consistently failed to get above freezing point and the frost was just about permanent. Games were being constantly rearranged and then postponed with clubs willing to play on any days except Sunday, which was still expressly forbidden thanks to the influence of the Church. Chelsea found a novel solution to the problem of keeping players match-fit; they played a friendly in Malta where the temperature was a scorching 16°C.

The FA Cup fourth round ties scheduled for Saturday, 26 January actually only featured one game from that round, although three third round matches did go ahead, though not Orient's. With 23 of the 32 third round ties not concluded, the FA had no choice but to postpone its traditional Monday lunchtime draw. The season was now likely to extend until at least 19 May – some way short of the 1946-47 record when the season was concluded on 14 June – hampered by a lack of floodlights to permit evening games. One other consequence of the weather was the introduction of the Pools Panel to artificially decide the results of matches. They sat for the first time today.

February saw no let up in the weather, indeed it seemed to deteriorate. On Saturday, 2 February only four Football League games went ahead, to equal the record of 12 January for the fewest number of League games played from a full schedule. By now, the backlog of League and Cup games had reached 385, the equivalent of eight Saturdays-worth of games.

Orient were due to play a home game against Burnley, but despite desperate measures being employed there was no need for fans to ring up the club and ask about the prospects of play. The maximum temperature reached during the day was -2°C. On one occasion the Orient groundsmen poured petrol all over the pitch, ignited it, and then dragged blankets across it to soak up the water. Even that couldn't melt the frost which had permeated deep into the pitch, but perhaps one should be grateful that Brisbane Road didn't end up getting burnt down to the ground with employees rushing around with their clothes on fire. Just imagine the reaction of the Health and Safety brigade if such a course of action were to be proposed today.

Saturday, 9 February was the eighth consecutive white-out for football, and Orient were once more denied the chance to play when their game at Sheffield Wednesday was postponed. The situation in London was easing, however, and the temperatures over the weekend just managed to stay above freezing, giving the Orient groundsmen a chance to work hard on the pitch. Their persistence paid off and, on the Monday, Orient played their first game of football in 47 days when their third round FA Cup-tie at home to Hull finally went ahead. The only change from that previous game, if supporters could remember that far back, was in goal, because Pinner was Cup-tied. George took his place. Fewer than 10,000 braved the bitter cold, the lowest attendance for a home FA Cup-tie since the war.

The Brisbane Road pitch was an unappealing mixture of mud and powdered snow, which turned the game into something of a lottery, with good football going out of the window. Hull managed to break the ice with a Chris Chilton rebound, but Musgrove rescued the home side from a giantkilling by whacking in an equaliser from 25 yards. 'Mine, mine, mine!' he yelled as he struck it, forcing his colleagues out of his way. Although Orient were happy to have avoided defeat, the last thing they wanted was a replay with such a huge backlog of matches already. At least they now knew the identity of their fourth round opponents if they prevailed, because Derby had beaten Peterborough 2-0 the week before.

Orient's League commitments restarted the following week as the weather conditions eased slightly, though most football matches were still off. There was a faint hope that the enforced break might work in Orient's favour, by breaking the cycle that had seen thirteen consecutive games without a win. Others had been hoping that winter would drag on for longer still, causing the League to abandon the rest of the season and declare that the 1962-63 fixtures would be replayed during 1963-64 – a forlorn hope.

The pressure to end that winless run was now overwhelming, because the visitors to Brisbane Road were the team occupying the other relegation place directly above Orient – Fulham. The Cottagers had a string of brilliant individuals contained within their team – Alan Mullery, Johnny Haynes, Bobby Robson and George Cohen, for example – but were not blending as a team. Orient had the opposite problem: they worked well as a unit, but lacked the individual talents of a truly top-class player who could consistently turn a game their way. Most Pools punters would have marked this game down as a banker draw on their coupons and the two teams duly obliged them – it ended 1-1.

Orient had outplayed Fulham in the first half, but fell behind early in the second half when Maurice Cook outjumped the centre-halves to head home. The lead didn't last long, as Deeley set off on one of his many sorties down the right wing and managed to find Graham with a low cross. He side-footed the ball in to ensure Orient gained their fourth consecutive home draw. Although draws weren't as expensive in those days, because there were only two points for a win, even so it was proving fatal to their survival hopes that they couldn't even win on their own patch. At least the previous season they had made up for poor home results by frequently winning away, but there was no joy to be had on away grounds this term, in the League at least.

The FA Cup replay at Hull took place on the Tuesday on a dreadful, snow-covered pitch. After 90 minutes the two sides had ground out an unconvincing goalless draw, with the most heat coming via a blazing row involving Cyril Lea that earned the argumentative player a booking. When the final whistle blew, and the prospect of extra-time became a reality, Orient's skipper Stan Charlton argued vehemently for an abandonment, perhaps partly because Hull were in the ascendancy at the time. His protests were brushed aside by both Hull's captain and the referee, countering that they had made it through three-quarters of the game already and the match went on. It was just as well, because a vicious shot from Musgrove and a delicate lob from Gibbs both found the back of the Hull net in this extra period and the Third Division side were out.

Graham and Gibbs gave the still-celebrating O's fans a nasty shock by slapping in transfer requests. Graham announced his intention of joining Notts County and for a while it appeared as though he would be allowed to leave. Gibbs was told that he would be staying. Whilst the wrangle was being sorted out, both players were dropped for the home game against Manchester City. Gibbs played in the reserves, whilst Graham had the day off. Elwood wouldn't have expected to step into the shoes of Graham if he had been fit, but most attention was focused on the reappearance of Lucas. The long hiatus had meant the Welsh international had only missed two League games, which must be a record for a player suffering a broken leg in mid-season.

Yet another rumour did the rounds about a transfer target for the bottom club, and it seemed to be a weekly occurrence, with every disaffected player being linked with them. This time it was inside-left

Jimmy McIlroy of Burnley. Whilst he was getting on a bit at 31, he would have undoubtedly been a creative strength at Brisbane Road. For once, the size of the fee wasn't a problem, it was the size of his pay packet. At £80 a week it was said that he would have been getting nearly twice the amount of the best paid O's player.

Fewer than 12,500 inside the Leyton Stadium at Brisbane Road proved that there wasn't a pent-up demand from the deprived fans to see football again; perhaps the glut of football matches was too much for the casuals.

Much more likely was the realisation that their side were unlikely to win, and much to everyone's chagrin they were proved right. The defence was strong enough to cope with Manchester City's rare excursions into their half and showed a willingness to come forward to help the attack, but the age-old failings were still there – a paucity of good-quality balls to the forwards and a lack of ruthlessness in front of goal. It's true that Orient did take the lead within a quarter of an hour, the tiny figure of Joe Elwood popping up like a jack-in-the-box to head home a cross by Bolland, but they never were able to add a second and third goal to kill off the game, not helped by Harry Dowd – a keeper in inspired form.

This left Orient exposed to the effects of an equalising fluke goal which the Citizens duly delivered twenty minutes later. Alex Harley's shot rebounded off keeper George like a ricocheting bullet and struck the inrushing City striker before he realised what was happening. The ball streaked into the net and the fifth consecutive scoring draw at Brisbane Road was a reality. They may not have been doing their own survival hopes any good, but at least they were doing their best to earn somebody a jackpot on the Pools.

	P	Pts
17 Bolton	22	19
18 Manchester C	23	19
19 Blackpool	24	19
20 Ipswich	25	18
21 Fulham	25	18
22 ORIENT	26	15

Orient needed to start winning games quickly to get themselves in amongst that pack of five clubs above them. Fulham had done exactly that by beating Nottingham Forest 3-1, but Blackpool and of course

Manchester City had also drawn to maintain their four-point advantage over the O's. They had a golden opportunity to take this important step when they played at Blackpool on 2 March.

Gibbs won back his place after his little spat with the club and it appears as though regular first-team action would keep him happy. Musgrove was unavailable due to an ankle injury sustained in the previous game and Carey took the opportunity to juggle positions slightly, most notably pushing Elwood wide out onto the wing. Not that it did any good. The Seasiders took the lead through an early penalty, awarded when Lea was spotted giving a little push to an opponent. A wicked deflection off Charlton gave Blackpool a second goal and John McPhee added a third midway through the second half. Orient did manage a late rally in the closing twenty minutes, courtesy of a Dunmore effort from distance and a Deeley penalty, but it was quite literally pointless.

Orient fans may have been resigned to relegation by now, but the FA Cup still gave them a faint hope that glory could be salvaged from the wreckage of their League form. A home tie against a Derby side who were looking possibilities for a drop into the Third Division gave even pessimistic Orientals hope of advancement. Season ticket holders were able to apply for stand seats a fortnight in advance, using vouchers, but in the end there was no need to panic for the tardy regulars who had left it late.

Just 12,607 watched the fourth round tie – a dreadful gate which must have made 'Happy' Harry Zussman drip tears onto his favourite giant cigars. Perhaps the Monday evening kick-off at 7.30pm put some people off, but usually even casual fans would turn up for an FA Cup game, even if it was played at three o'clock in the morning.

A tremendous game of football rewarded the meagre crowd. The home element were cheered by an early goal from Dunmore who managed to out-sprint a trio of Derby defenders before turning rapidly to smack in another of his medium distance bazookas. Derby had plenty of chances to level, but it was satisfying to see another team riddled with self-doubts in front of goal for a change and all they managed was to give the fans behind the Orient goal some catching practise. Robertson was a rare sight in goal, but the 37-year-old third-choice keeper (George was injured and Pinner Cup-tied) was given a gentle workout.

O's supporters indulged in synchronised nail-biting up until the last twenty minutes of the game, when Elwood flung himself amongst the flailing boots to make it 2-0, and Deeley made it three just before the referee's last whistle of the night.

Orient were granted their third consecutive home tie of the season in the FA Cup draw, but Leicester City were far more difficult opponents than Hull or Derby. They were still putting in a credible League title bid and were level on points with leaders Tottenham, and they had some Cup pedigree too, having reached the final in 1961.

Orient had just fifteen games left in Division One to save themselves, and being as they hadn't won in sixteen games it was going to need something special to give them hope. That came with the signature of 26-year-old inside-forward Bobby Mason. He had been involved in a bitter dispute with Wolverhampton Wanderers that had its origins in the decision to drop him for the 1960 FA Cup final. The disgruntled star, who had been a firm favourite with the Molineux fans, sensationally walked out on them to join non-league Chelmsford City. With no hope of a return to Wolves, who still retained his registration, but still desperate for top-class football, he was persuaded to join Orient. As part of the £15,000 deal, Orient allowed reserve centre-forward Bob Grant to head in the opposite direction. Grant had been signed from Carlisle at the beginning of the season, but the Scot was obviously never going to get a game for Orient, despite their woes in front of goal.

Mason was billed as 'Our Great Saviour' and made his debut on Saturday, 9 March at home to Aston Villa, though his presence did nothing to swell the crowd, which actually fell by 1,000. Although the transfer deadline had been extended from 15 March to 6 April, there was little prospect of any more signings.

The club alluded to this in the match programme by hitting back at their critics who had wanted new faces to appear more quickly. The club stated that the right players weren't easily found because transfer fees were exorbitant and Orient's cash-flow as a result of the big freeze had hindered them still further. There was still every likelihood that Graham was going to be sold, but Notts County were no longer linked with him. Luton Town were the new favourites to capture him.

Mason had a reasonable debut, though some felt his exile with Chelmsford had dulled his abilities. Villa had the benefits of a gale-force wind behind them in the first half and they took advantage by scoring twice. After six minutes left-back Lewis conceded an indirect free-kick and was duly booked for giving the referee a frank opinion on the validity of the decision. The resulting free-kick carried in the wind and was met by the diving figure of Phil Woosnam, a former captain of the Orient side. That goal was matched by another just before half-time and even the goalkeeper nearly made it three when his clearance bounced over the head of his opposite number Robertson, but just went wide of the goal.

Orient failed to do anything of note in the second half, despite the benefits of the wind and driving rain that stung the faces of the Villains. The bored Orient fans amused themselves with a game of 'Spot The Grass' in the ploughed field that the pitch resembled.

CHAPTER SEVEN

So Long, Farewell,
Auf Wiedersehen, Adieu

(March-May 1963)

Orient secretary George Hicks asked the police if he could increase the capacity of Brisbane Road from 31,000 to 35,000 for the visit of Leicester City in the fifth round of the FA Cup. Though the O's were bidding to reach the quarter-finals for the third time in their history (1926 and 1954 were the previous occasions), in the end his pleas were pointless because only 25,759 turned up. A large number of these were visiting fans, borne on 150 coaches, four special trains and innumerable cars.

Mason didn't play in this game as he had turned out for Chelmsford in FA Cup games this season and the rules didn't allow players to turn out for two different clubs in the competition during the same season. Musgrove celebrated his election as the chairman of the Professional Footballers' Association by returning to the left-wing position. The PFA role was a great honour for Musgrove, his status as a qualified coach helping to secure his new post.

For the third consecutive Saturday, Orient succumbed to a goal scored after six minutes. A brilliant 40-yard run by City's right-winger Howard Riley drew most players towards the ball, leaving Ken Keyworth alone in the centre to accept the gift of his sweetly hit cross. Orient battled gamely to get back on level terms, but their passing game was often ineffective as the ball fought a personal battle against the mud.

Leicester used longer balls with great accuracy. Although they never had as much possession as their opponents, they still managed to hit the crossbar twice. Deeley was Orient's man-of-the-match, jinking down the right wing past the left-back and providing crosses that nobody could convert. Orient fans thought they had found salvation when the hulking figure of Lewis put all his considerable weight into a header just before the end, but though keeper Gordon Banks was beaten, defender John Sjoberg leapt up on the line to head clear. It was the only time Banks was beaten, his bravery and agility winning him grudging respect from the home fans.

The 0-1 defeat cost Orient the chance of a winnable-looking trip to Second Division Norwich City, but it was Leicester who duly took advantage of that, going on to reach the final, which had been put back to 25 May. They lost 1-3 to Manchester United.

With only the last third of the League season to look forward to, the fans were now weary, frustrated and angry in equal measure. One supporter even went as far as ringing up coach Eddie Baily and telling him he'd got 4,000 names on a petition, urging the club to sign new players. Baily responded by asking the guy to bring it round so he could sign it too, and then he'd get all the directors to add their signatures as well. Baily also added that they'd be better off signing rugby players in view of the dire straits they were in.

Mason regained his place and Elwood was dropped, but no matter what Carey did, a League victory was still a seemingly impossible dream. Orient hung on for 54 minutes in the home game against Nottingham Forest before the effects of mud and Colin Addison's boot combined to give the visitors a 1-0 win. Orient were finding it much more difficult to penetrate the defences of even mediocre First Division sides like Forest, though they had hardly been prolific even in the Second Division promotion season.

O's fans finally got to trot across to North London for the game at Spurs, the most attractive side in British football. Many people with no clear-cut allegiances to any one side would have switched to watching Tottenham regularly, though plenty of diehard Orientals found it impossible to resist the allure of White Hart Lane when Orient weren't playing.

The crowd of 40,260 was the largest to witness Orient playing a game in London, beating the previous record of 36,500 at West Ham in 1957. The record is now 49,698 for the FA Cup semi-final against Arsenal at neutral Stamford Bridge in 1978.

Orient certainly didn't embarrass themselves on this Wednesday night and they weren't afraid to take the game to Tottenham. The one difference that separated the sides being the quality of the attacks. Orient's failings have been well documented, but Spurs had two of the best centre-forwards anyone could possibly hope for. Bobby Smith and Jimmy Greaves were both England internationals and Orient would probably have finished in mid-table with a pair of strikers like that. Smith was the archetypal barnstorming centre-forward of yore and he had already shaken the post twice before making it third time lucky midway through the first half.

Greaves was the jinking goal-poacher supreme and the only way the harassed Lea could stop him was by a clumsy two-footed tackle from behind in the second half. That earned Lea a booking and Greaves one of the 357 First Division goals of his career from the resulting penalty-kick.

Lea had played in 105 consecutive League games, but injury prevented him from adding to that total for the 30 March trip up to Wolves. Gibbs took his place, but the attention of the 13,000 Wolves fans was focused on two of their former players. Deeley was given a standing ovation, but Mason would probably have been strung up from the crossbar if they could have had their way.

Neither of them were able to inflict any damage on their former club, even though Deeley looked a cert to score from three yards, but still fired over the bar. Graham did at least manage to end the sad run of his club's four goalless games, with an effort five minutes into the second half, but by then his side were already two goals down and destined to lose yet again. The defeat left Orient six points adrift of Birmingham and Manchester City and their rivals had played three fewer games too.

	P	Pts
19 Ipswich	32	22
20 Birmingham	28	21
21 Manchester C	28	21
22 ORIENT	31	15

Orient should have played their home League game with Leicester on 29 December, but it took until 3 April to fulfil the fixture. The club were re-using the original programme, but deliberately leaving the date on the front cover blank.

The 'goals for' column would also be blank for this game, because not only did nobody score, nobody looked like scoring. Leicester had no such troubles and a couple of first-half headers from Mike Stringfellow decided the outcome. The better weather had encouraged some of the fans to return, though Orient's hapless performance did nothing to keep them coming back for more.

Orient had been due to meet Liverpool at home on Saturday, 5 April, but it clashed with the clinching Home International Championship match between England and Scotland at Wembley. Liverpool had Gerry Byrne and Jimmy Melia in the England side and Ian St John turning out for Scotland, so the match was postponed, much to Orient's irritation. They would have loved to have played an under-strength Liverpool side.

Scottish Second Division side Morton were similarly at a loose end, so they travelled down to Leyton to play a friendly on the Friday night. Carey decided to stick with his first-choice defensive line-up, which included Mike Pinner, who had won his place back in goal since the Tottenham game. Dunmore and Mason retained their places, but Gregory and Elwood were given a rare run-out.

One new face in the first team was teenage centre-forward Micky Hollow – a low-key signing from Bishop's Stortford in the summer. He scored one of the goals in the 4-0 victory over the Scottish Second Division promotion-hopefuls, but his dreams of a quick call-up to top-class action were subsequently dashed. He did appear the following season, but by then he had been converted to a left-back. The other goals came from Dunmore, Elwood (though helped by a classic Scottish goalkeeping howler) and an own-goal. Being as it was a friendly, both sides allowed a substitute to come on and Gibbs replaced Charlton for Orient.

All three Easter games were against sides fearful of relegation too, so if a miracle was going to happen three victories were required. Bolton visited Leyton on Good Friday and, like their opponents, only had a solitary away win to their credit in the League. Elwood's strong performance in the Morton friendly won him a place at Musgrove's expense and Lea and Gregory were also present, replacing Gibbs and Deeley.

It didn't change a thing. For the seventh time in a row Orient lost a League game. Embarrassingly they failed to score, even when Bolton's goalkeeper was off the field for eighteen minutes following a collision with his own centre-half. Left-back Syd Farrimond took his place and made a couple of superb saves to deny Dunmore and Gregory. When the hobbling keeper returned to the action, Orient were doomed. The killer goal came halfway through the second half. Lewis tried to play a typical short ball out of defence, steered it to the intercepting Ron Davies instead, and then compounded his error by chopping down the striker in the box. The penalty was dispatched and the game was lost.

With a trip to Ipswich the next day there was no time to dwell on the defeat, though Carey was quick to replace the distraught Lewis at left-back, whilst Musgrove played the lone striker's role with Dunmore operating just behind him. Bolland was also present, but if the changes were designed to make Orient an attacking force they failed miserably. Musgrove did manage a sweetly struck goal from twenty yards, but that was nullified by an equaliser from Dougie Moran. Both sides otherwise demonstrated why they deserved to be in the Second Division the following season and there was little joy to be gleaned amongst the 18,678 crowd.

There was embarrassment in the Orient dressing room as well as on the pitch. Stan Charlton was standing on the bench, looking out through the unfrosted top part of the window at a quaint little garden on the other side. He spied an attractive lady in the garden and informed the other players that he would like to get better acquainted with her, though he may have put it a bit more graphically than that. Naturally the other players had a peek, but Charlton's face turned a redder shade of beetroot when Mike Pinner informed him that it was his wife he was referring to.

On Easter Monday, 15 April, Orient made the long train ride up for the return meeting with Bolton. Graham came back in place of Bolland, but that cannot explain why Orient's forward line suddenly clicked into gear. For once they looked dangerous throughout the 90 minutes and more importantly they scored. Elwood created the goal brilliantly by a clever back-pass to Dunmore who eagerly snapped up the gift.

Bolton's attack was subdued and finally the O's had a League win under their belt for the first time in 24 attempts. The previous win had been way back on 29 September (at Fulham), though it did little to improve the look of the League table, especially as the three sides immediately above them all picked up a point.

	P	Pts
19 Manchester U	32	26
20 Manchester C	33	26
21 Birmingham	32	25
22 ORIENT	35	18

The two Manchester clubs were the safety target, but even if those clubs averaged around a point every other game, Orient were doomed, because the Londoners would only get to 32 points with seven straight wins, which was not a credible scenario.

The O's fans thought so too, because a tiny crowd of 8,274 turned up for the visit of Blackburn. Orient did well to rescue a point from the proceedings, gleaned when Dunmore delicately steered in Mason's cross after 58 minutes. That was after Rovers had taken the lead through Fred Pickering after fourteen minutes, though Pinner's mist-imed dive helped him enormously. The 1-1 draw narrowed the gap on Birmingham, who lost 3-6 at home to Blackpool, but the Manchester sides did well enough to ensure they only needed two more wins to send Orient effectively down.

A Friday-night visit to mid-table Sheffield United gave Orient a chance of winning, because United's manager John Harris had four teenagers in his line-up, with two making their debut. All four of them were little diamonds though, and went on to become heroes at Bramall Lane. Len Badger and Bernard Shaw were the full-backs making their first starts, whilst Tony Wagstaff and Mick Jones brought youthful threats to their front line.

The exuberance of these players ran rings round the more mature visitors and Jones bagged his third goal in three matches with a superb header, similar to the many he was to score at Leeds United from 1967 onwards. Barry Hartle may have been an old-timer at 23 in comparison, but he still had more energy than poor Stan Charlton (33) and he sprinted past him to deliver the second goal. The pain of the 0-2 defeat was slightly tempered the following day when Birmingham lost 1-6 at Blackburn, and Manchester City were thrashed 1-5 at home by West Brom.

With relegation almost a certainty, secretary George Hicks announced that season tickets would be the same price for next season – £8 8s (£8.40) or £9 9s (£9.45) – depending on where in the ground you were. This was still more than the last time they were in the Second Division as they had raised their prices for the First Division campaign. Hicks said that although they expected expenditure to be the same, they were still looking for new players to get them back into the First Division. Carey predicted that a seventeen-year-old bank clerk in Orient's successful South-East Counties side would have a bright future. He was right. Goalkeeper Peter Vasper did, but not until he had joined Norwich City in 1968.

The trip to Sheffield United should have been Orient's last game of the season, but there were still five postponed matches to wade through. A Thursday in May was an unusual time to see the O's playing a home game, and only 8,273 – the lowest gate of the season – came to see their penultimate Brisbane Road appearance as a top-flight outfit. Top-scorer Dunmore was dropped, with Graham taking his place, but the front men seemed to work extra hard as a result of Dunmore's absence and two goals were scored in a three-minute spell after a quarter of an hour.

Graham joyously slammed in a 25-yard shot after beating two men to make room for himself, whilst Bishop hared forward to play a one-two with Musgrove and score his first goal for the club in over two years. Liverpool pulled a goal back before half-time. But Orient hung on gamely to end their sequence of fourteen home games without a win. Fittingly the last win had been against Liverpool's great rivals Everton.

Saturday, 4 May was originally FA Cup final day, but that had been put back three weeks. Instead it became Orient's date with destiny, for if they failed to beat Sheffield Wednesday then relegation would be confirmed. Orient bounced back after conceding a first-half goal and Graham levelled with a header. Wednesday gradually wore down their opponents in the second period though, and two further goals sent Orient down whence they came.

	P	Pts
18 Manchester U	38	31
19 Bolton	39	31
20 Birmingham	38	29
21 Manchester C	38	28
22 ORIENT	39	21

Although Orient's final home game as a First Division club drew only 10,085 to Brisbane Road, the fans made up for the lack of numbers with a increase in the volume levels. They yearned to see an Orient victory, but Burnley weren't in a charitable mood and they sneaked a victory when George failed to get down quickly enough to a shot. Orient couldn't even manage a goal, even when Elwood was presented with the easiest of efforts near the end, but perhaps the game summed up the whole of Orient's season.

With relegation now official, Carey announced that five players would be given free transfers. Three were goalkeepers – Frank George, Bill Robertson and Albert Cochran. Roger Wedge hadn't done enough to convince Carey he was worth retaining, whilst left-back Roy Deakes had never even made the first team. The other 21 players were retained, but Carey was cagey on his team's chances for next season, jokingly stating that they hadn't finished this one yet. The fans aired their views more readily and most of them were astute enough to realise that promotion back to the First was unlikely, without a major change of personnel. Even the famous half-back line of Lucas, Lea and Bishop was not going to be part of the future for much longer, not if everyone was realistic.

Carey was absent for the short trip to West Ham in the penultimate game, preferring to make the longer trip to Scotland to eye up a potential Oriental for next season. He didn't miss anything worth seeing at Upton Park. His side were well beaten by a team that hardly seemed to be bothering to move out of first gear. They killed the game off with a goal in each half, the second being a spectacular overhead kick from Tony Scott that was a rare highlight in the match. A large chunk of the sparse crowd of 16,746 was made up of Orient fans who congregated behind one of the goals and roared on the team in a rare display of noisiness.

Even Orient fans were aware that there wasn't a great deal of singing done at Brisbane Road, but away fans are naturally more dedicated and therefore more passionate. They sung 'The O's Go Marching On' and the old standard 'Dear Old Pals'. They at least were going to stay loyal to their beloved team, even though they realised that the glorious promotion campaign wasn't likely to be replicated in the near future and that as a consequence meetings with the big glamour clubs were going to be reserved for the occasional cup games once again. Even though the season in the top flight had been one of almost unremitting disappointment, they wouldn't have swapped it for anything. Just to see the very best teams that English football could offer on a weekly basis, pitching themselves up against their team, made the heartache worthwhile (almost).

The season signed off on Saturday, 18 May 1963 with a visit to one of the most charismatic teams in the division in one of the most imposing stadiums. Manchester United may have always been high on the list of the most entertaining teams and they were always one of the sides who would be fancied to do well, but frequently they under-performed and this season more than most. They were still fearful of joining Orient in the Second Division the following season and could not afford to relax.

To complicate matters they were in next week's FA Cup final (against Leicester) and their players must have had a maelstrom of emotions whizzing through their heads as they simultaneously played for their places in the game's showcase, whilst playing for their footballing futures.

	P	Pts
19 Manchester U	40	32
20 Birmingham	41	31
21 Manchester C	41	31
22 ORIENT	41	21

Once more a terribly low crowd barely filled half of the ground, which goes to show that football crowds weren't necessarily larger in those days. In the 21st Century, even the most minor of games at Old Trafford would attract an attendance far in excess of the 32,759 that appeared on this day, let alone a fixture that had so much riding upon it.

It was a truism that Orient tended to play better against the sides that played the type of passing game that they too tried to emulate. They had already beaten the Red Devils at home during the same week that they had whipped the eventual League champions Everton 3-0. The O's looked as though they wanted to relive those glory days when they took an early lead. Dave Dunmore was the goalscorer, his strike ensuring that he matched Graham's total of fourteen League and Cup goals for the season, though Dunmore was ahead in terms of League goals scored (eleven to nine).

Orient clung on valiantly until the last ten minutes, when United finally discovered a sense of urgency about the situation. A 25-year-old Bobby Charlton raced down the pitch and let fly with a shot, and though it lacked the venom of many of his spectacular strikes down the years, it was still good enough to fool goalkeeper George, especially when it hit the head of the other Charlton on the pitch – Orient's Stan. Denis Law then showed off some of his magic to put them ahead 30 seconds later, something which Orient's master-men had done too little of this season. Bobby Charlton finished off the game and virtually sealed their survival hopes by banging in another sweet shot, this time unaided by any part of an Oriental's anatomy. To make United hearts lift that extra mile, results elsewhere confirmed that neighbours City would be joining Orient in Division Two next season.

And so Orient's top-flight career came to a swift end and the inquests delivered their verdicts. Like so many managers down the years, Carey had given the promotion side the chance to prove themselves up to the tasks expected of them. This may have been partly down to sentimentality, but pragmatism played a major part as he knew he could not indulge in a major rebuilding exercise. With that most wonderful of all gifts – hindsight – it is easy to see that Carey should have been more ruthless in axing some of the players not quite good enough for the step up and that the board should have leaned more heavily on their wealthier directors and showbusiness associates to find the funds to replace them, but recklessness could have resulted in long-term financial difficulties or even bankruptcy, with no guarantees of surviving the drop anyway.

Orient's defence had been as strong as it had been the season before and the total of 81 goals conceded is more of a mark of the problems further up the field than of any failings at the back. The attack received the bulk of the criticism throughout both seasons, in terms of creating chances, holding the ball up waiting for support, and especially in sticking the ball in the net. Their goals total of 37 was the lowest in the First Division since Birmingham's 31 in 1949-50. To put it into perspective, Orient's 81 goals conceded was only four worse than Arsenal who finished seventh, and far better than Birmingham's 90 or Manchester City's 102.

Perhaps less reliance on the push-and-run style, with a greater emphasis on mixing it up with more long balls might have helped the O's survive, but Carey and Baily were perhaps the best ones to judge the best way of getting the best out of their players. It's definitely true that the eventual signings of Mason and Musgrove came too late and perhaps players of similar quality could have been found earlier. But perhaps to find the real reason for their relative failure one needs to go back another season. Everything came together beautifully during the Second Division promotion season. Their squad of talented players peaked at just the right time, helped by that incredible injury-free start. Had an occasional injury been suffered by key players in that charmed period then it is perfectly feasible that Orient would have finished in mid-table. Perhaps it is the case that Orient had done as well as they could have done in the First Division, given the fact that they had spectacularly over-performed in the Second.

Orient deserved a bit of glory to come their way for giving it their all, and Stan Charlton earned it by receiving the *Walthamstow Guardian*'s

'Sportsman of the Year' award for 1962, for leading his team into the
First Division. A fitting tribute to the player and a strong reflection on
the glorious promotion side.

The Slide Back into the Third Division

Carey now stated that he was starting on a new era of team rebuilding, with an emphasis on youth ahead of experience, driven by the knowledge that many of the stars of the past few years were now feeling a decline in their abilities. The first to express a desire to leave was Mal Graham and in July 1963 he signed for Third Division QPR, along with Derek Gibbs, for a joint fee of £10,000. Graham stayed with Rangers for a year before moving back to his native Yorkshire to join Barnsley. He stayed with them for a season and is still living in the town.

Gibbs had a couple of seasons at Loftus Road before joining Romford in 1965. He helped them to the Southern League title in 1966-67 and then had spells with Hastings United, Wealdstone and Dunstable. He was still playing football in the 1970s, but has since retired to the East Sussex coast.

Orient's two long-serving custodians of the net also left Orient in the close season. Frank George joined Watford, where he was understudy to the exciting teenage goalkeeper Pat Jennings. George joined Worcester in 1965 after only ten games for Watford's first team, but suffered a serious injury whilst with the Southern League outfit which prompted his retirement from football. He is now living in London.

Bill Robertson also moved into the Southern League, this time with Dover. He died in Tadworth in Surrey in June 1973 at the ridiculously young age of 44, the first of the promotion side to pass away.

A twice-broken leg finished David Clark's Orient playing career, but he became a trainer at Brisbane Road before losing his job in Orient's financial crisis in 1966. There is no truth in the rumour that he started the Dave Clark Five.

Bill Taylor initially stayed with Orient, but didn't play any games for the first team again. He moved to Nottingham Forest in October 1963 and stayed for nearly six years, though he only played 21 League games for them. He joined Lincoln City in May 1969, making 79 League appearances and two years later joined Fulham as reserve-team coach under manager Alec Stock, his old Orient boss. He progressed to coaching the first team and was rewarded when his charges made the 1975 FA Cup final, though they lost to West Ham. In October 1975 he started coaching the England side and he remained part of that set-up for the rest of his life. He became Manchester City's assistant manager in May 1976 under Tony Book and in July 1979 became Oldham's first-team coach. He was still coaching for club and country when he suffered a viral infection in 1981. This attacked his nervous system and he went into a coma and died. He was only just into his forties.

The only new player who featured in Orient's first game back in the Second Division was ex-Arsenal wing-half Gerry Ward, and for most of the season it was the old guard who turned out in the blue jerseys. The old failings in attack were also familiar though, and they finished in the bottom half of the table with only 54 goals scored. The famed defence was also on the wane and they took a few hammerings on the way, losing 3-6 at home to Portsmouth and 2-5 at home to Sunderland.

By this time they were being managed by Benny Fenton, because Johnny Carey had also left soon after their relegation. He became manager of Nottingham Forest in 1963, staying there for five years and keeping them in the First Division throughout. He even took them back into the Fairs Cup in 1967-68. In 1970 he rejoined Blackburn Rovers as manager after an absence of twelve years, but didn't stay very long as they tumbled towards the Third Division for the first time in their history. He died in August 1995 at the age of 76.

Another clearout of Orient's relegation side took place by the end of that 1963-64 season. Bobby Mason joined Poole Town in March 1964 and later had a spell back at Chelmsford City. He then moved to the relative backwaters of Parley Sports near Bournemouth and he still lives in the area. A few years ago he once more featured in the headlines due to a bizarre story. A doppelganger went around telling everyone that he was Bobby Mason – the ex-Wolves and Orient player. He fooled a lot of people and even the woman he married was convinced he was the ex-football star. Eventually, of course, the secret emerged and the real Bobby Mason was able to stand up to prove that this other fellow was an impostor.

Eddie Lewis left to join yet another Southern League outfit – Folkestone Town. He later managed Ford Sports and Clapton before emigrating to South Africa in 1970. He worked for a family garden-service company there, but also got heavily involved in football in various capacities, including managership. He was part of South Africa's technical team for the 1998 World Cup in France and became a respected football commentator for the programme *Top Sport*. He lives in Johannesburg and still keenly follows the fortunes of Manchester United and Leyton Orient.

Norman Deeley joined Leicester City in July 1964, but never played for their first team. He moved to Bromsgrove Rovers in August 1967 and Darlaston in September 1971. He is now a matchday host at Walsall.

Gordon Bolland was another part of this stampede and he was sold to Norwich City in March 1964. He made a century of League appearances for them before a brief spell with Charlton in 1967-68. In October 1968 he moved to Millwall and in seven seasons became an extremely popular member of their team, scoring 62 League goals in 244 games. A hip injury meant he moved back to his native Boston and he was manager of the local team for a while. He later became a director there, but is currently enjoying the quiet life, as he puts it.

The 1964-65 season finally saw the smashing-up of that legendary Lucas-Bishop-Lea half-back line. Mal Lucas left in September 1964 after failing to see eye-to-eye with manager Benny Fenton. He joined Norwich for £15,000 in a player-exchange with Colin Worrell. He attained legendary status at Carrow Road over the course of 183 League appearances before joining Torquay United in March 1970. He made another century of League appearances there before moving back to Norfolk and undergoing a series of jobs, including a few in the Great Yarmouth holiday trade. He managed four local sides – Lowestoft, Gorleston, Hoveton and Wroxham – and has now retired and is living in Norwich.

Cyril Lea earned the O's £20,000 when he moved to Ipswich in November 1964. He was another player who made over 100 appearances for his new club and finally managed to win some long-deserved international honours too, turning out for Wales for a couple of games in 1965. He also coached the national side and fulfilled a similar role at Ipswich too. In August 1979 he became assistant manager at Stoke and performed the same role at Hull City. In 1983 he became sole manager of Colchester United for three years, though he could never quite lift them out of the Fourth Division. He left them to become Youth Development Officer at Leicester City and youth coach at West Brom. His last footballing job was chief scout at Rushden & Diamonds.

Sid Bishop played in the reserves for a short while, but was released by new manager Dave Sexton in 1965. He was player-manager at both Hastings and Guildford City, before running a pub in Portsmouth for a while. He is now living in Essex.

Phil White's Orient career ended sadly. Having sustained a serious leg injury during the promotion season, he never played for the first team in the First Division. He made a brief comeback in October 1964, but was never the same player he once was. The club staged a benefit for him in June 1964, but he passed away in June 2000.

Stan Charlton left in 1965 and became player-manager of Weymouth for seven years, helping them to the Southern League Championship on the way. In 1988 he became secretary of the club for four years and he is now their Life Vice-President. He also made a lot of people very happy by working for Vernons Pools for seven years as an area manager. Orient gave him a benefit match in April 1970 and he also managed the Dorset County side. He still lives in that area.

Mike Pinner was also released when Dave Sexton became the manager in January 1965, mostly because the new boss didn't like the idea of having a part-timer on the staff. Pinner continued working as a solicitor during the week, but on Saturday mornings would catch a flight to Belfast in order to play for Distillery, returning home the same evening. He has now retired as a solicitor and is living in London.

Terry McDonald joined Reading in May 1965, becoming a stalwart of their Football Combination side and helping them to that championship. He later had spells with Wimbledon and Folkestone and also had a period of time in the USA running soccer clinics. He coached youngsters at Chelsea and has run several betting shops, mostly in Hornchurch, but also at Great Portland Street in London. He is never allowed to forget about his magical winning goal against Manchester United whenever he bumps into long-standing Orient fans.

Dave Dunmore left Orient in June 1965 after cracking in 54 League goals in 147 games. He joined York for a couple of seasons before signing for Wellington Town in 1967 (later to be known as Telford United). He now lives in York.

With so many great players leaving and Orient lacking the resources to adequately replace them, it was inevitable that the club's fortunes would decline. Benny Fenton's year-long spell in charge ended with the club balancing precariously on the edge of the relegation zone as the affable boss sought to change the style of the team into one which might have been less pretty, but which would be more effective.

Essentially this was a variation on the Ipswich style of the late-1950s and early 60s with unorthodox deep-lying wingers, and to emphasise the point he even recruited the on-the-pitch architect of that team – Ted Phillips.

Dave Sexton was only 34 when he was appointed – a younger generation than either Carey or Fenton – and his fresh ideas involved clearing out most of the old guard and bringing in new talent, though the lack of funds available precluded most of his ambitious plans. They did manage to avoid relegation in 1964-65, but only by two points, and the following season was an unmitigated disaster reminiscent of their First Division foray. Sexton resigned in December 1965 with only three League wins under his belt and Les Gore was drafted in for his sixth and final spell as a caretaker manager. There was nothing he could do. The club won only two away games and finished ten points adrift at the foot of the Second Division. By then their average League gates had plummeted and in one game at home to Middlesbrough they only attracted a gate of 2,286. This brought enormous financial repercussions and the club very nearly went bankrupt in 1966, only saving themselves with the generosity of several patrons, most famously at a meeting in November 1966 when a bucket was passed round and duly filled with cash. Harry Zussman stepped down as chairman, though he remained with the club until his death in July 1981. To signify the new start, the club dropped their 'Leyton' prefix and became known just as 'Orient'. They also switched to an all-red strip, partly at the request of the Football League, who were concerned about the huge number of teams that played in blue.

None of the members of the glory team of 1961-63 had to suffer the ignominy of playing in the Third Division. Joe Elwood moved back to Northern Ireland in June 1966 and played for Ards. He later moved back to London, working as a PE teacher for a couple of schools in Homerton. He is still a regular at Orient matches and also retains the distinction of being the first ever substitute for Orient in a Football League game when he replaced James McGeorge in September 1965.

Malcolm Musgrove was a player-coach at Orient in 1964-65, but left to fulfil a number of coaching and management roles at a dizzying number of clubs, including Charlton, Aston Villa, Leicester, Manchester United, Torquay, Exeter and Plymouth. He became a leading light in American soccer and also helped Qatar's national side.

Last to leave was Harry Gregory, who joined Charlton in August 1966. He made over 150 appearances for the Haddicks and joined

Aston Villa in October 1970. In August 1972 he joined the Football League's newest club, Hereford United, and helped them to promotion in their first season. He now lives in the London area.

This book very nearly had an extra few chapters. In 1969-70 Orient returned to the Second Division as champions and in 1973-74 came within a point of a glorious return back to Division One. Whereas in 1961-62 they had profited from a long spell without injuries, conversely this time round they faltered with a cruel run of injuries in the late winter. They would have still gone up had they won their final game at home to Aston Villa, but a 1-1 draw allowed Carlisle United their one and only 'Season in the Sun'.

At the time of publication Orient had just been promoted from the basement and although an ascent towards the Premiership seems very unlikely, I hope that one day their might be a sequel to this book.

Guide to Seasonal Summaries

Col 1: Match number (for league fixtures); Round (for cup-ties).
e.g. 4R means 'Fourth round replay.'

Col 2: Date of the fixture and whether Home (H), Away (A), or Neutral (N).

Col 3: Opposition.

Col 4: Attendances. Home gates appear in roman; Away gates in *italics*.
Figures in **bold** indicate the largest and smallest gates, at home and away.
Average home and away attendances appear after the final league match.

Col 5: Respective league positions of Orient and opponents after the game.
Orient's position appears on the top line in roman.
Their opponents' position appears on the second line in *italics*.
For cup-ties, the division and position of opponents is provided.
e.g. 2:12 means the opposition are twelfth in Division 2.

Col 6: The top line shows the result: W(in), D(raw), or L(ose).
The second line shows Orient's cumulative points total.

Col 7: The match score, Orient's given first.
Scores in **bold** show Orient's biggest league win and heaviest defeat.

Col 8: The half-time score, Orient's given first.

Col 9: The top line shows Orient's scorers and times of goals in roman.
The second line shows opponents' scorers and times of goals in *italics*.
A 'p' after the time of a goal denotes a penalty; 'og' an own-goal.
The third line gives the name of the match referee.

Team line-ups: Orient line-ups appear on top line, irrespective of whether
they are home or away. Opposition teams are on the second line in *italics*.
Players of either side who are sent off are marked !
Orient players making their league debuts are displayed in **bold**

LEAGUE DIVISION 2

Manager: Johnny Carey

SEASON 1961-62

Match results (Pos = Orient position + result; Opp Pos = printed "Pos" column)

No	Date	Venue	Opponents	Pos	Att	Opp Pos	Pt	F-A	H-T	Scorers, Times, and Referees
1	19/8	A	Newcastle	9 D	26,638	10	1	0-0	0-0	Ref: L Hamer
2	21/8	H	Southampton	15 L	12,479	7	1	1-3	0-1	Foster 55; O'Brien 28, Mulgrew 62, 77; Ref: L Callaghan
3	26/8	H	Middlesbrough	11 W	9,269	21	3	2-0	1-0	White 4, Lucas 85; Ref: T Dawes
4	30/8	A	Southampton	7 W	14,352	18	5	2-1	0-0	Foster 76, McDonald 85; O'Brien 52; Ref: D Smith
5	2/9	A	Walsall	3 W	15,963	8	7	5-1	2-0	Foster 5, Dunm' 43, Graham 63, 75, 77; Younger 80; Ref: R Smith
6	9/9	H	Derby	2 W	12,316	9	9	2-0	1-0	Swallow 37 (og), Dunmore 53p; Ref: J Osborne
7	16/9	A	Bristol Rov	4 L	11,824	22	9	1-2	0-1	Dunmore 76p; Hooper 6, Jones 69; Ref: W Clements
8	20/9	H	Huddersfield	2 W	9,957	10	11	3-0	2-0	McDonald 24, Foster 26, Graham 52; Ref: G Pullin
9	23/9	A	Preston	4 L	9,956	21	11	2-3	0-1	McDonald 75, Foster 77; Thompson 3, Biggs 50, Humes 62; Ref: E Crawford
10	27/9	A	Huddersfield	4 D	16,917	6	12	1-1	1-0	White 39; Bettany 87; Ref: K Walker

Orient line-up (unchanged for all ten matches):

1	2	3	4	5	6	7	8	9	10	11
George	Charlton	Lewis	Lucas	Bishop	Lea	White	Foster	Dunmore	Graham	McDonald

Opposition line-ups:

No	Opponents	1	2	3	4	5	6	7	8	9	10	11
1	Newcastle	Hollins	Keith	McMichael	Neale	McGrath	Bell	Hughes	Harrower	McGuigan	Allchurch	Tuohy
2	Southampton	Godfrey	Davies	Traynor	Clifton	Knapp	Huxford	Paine	O'Brien	Reeves	Mulgrew	Sydenham
3	Middlesbrough	Appleby	Jones	McNeil	Yeoman	Thomson	Harner	Day	Harris	Livingstone	Peacock	Holliday
4	Southampton	Godfrey	Davies	Patrick	Clifton	Knapp	Huxford	Paine	O'Brien	Reeves	Mulgrew	Sydenham
5	Walsall	Christie	Palin	Partridge	Hill	McPherson	Dudley	Askey	Hodgkisson	Wilson	Younger	Taylor
6	Derby	Oxford	Conwell	Davies	Parry	Young	Hopkinson	Roby	Powell	Thompson	Hutchinson	Swallow
7	Bristol Rov	Radford	Hills	Frowen	Mabbutt	Pyle	Slocombe	Petherbridge	Sykes	Bradford	Jones	Hooper
8	Huddersfield	Fearnley	Parker	Wilson	Saward	Coddington	Dinsdale	McHale	Kerray	Stokes	Massie	O'Grady
9	Preston	Kelly	Rose	O'Neill	Wylie	Singleton	Smith	Humes	Biggs	Alston	Sneddon	Thompson
10	Huddersfield	Fearnley	Atkins	Wilson	Saward	Parker	Dinsdale	McHale	Kerray	Stokes	Bettany	O'Grady

Match reports:

1. Newcastle are back in the Second Division after an absence of 13 years, but on this showing they are in for an extended stay. Orient would have won with a little more confidence, but they play well with left-winger McDonald always looking lively. A good solid start to the season.

2. Although Foster manages to head in from a corner kick to equalise, Southampton's lively forwards prove too much, despite getting regularly caught in Orient's offside trap. A fourth goal is only prevented by a rugby tackle by Lea on O'Brien which earns him a booking and a booing.

3. Despite gaining an early advantage when White strokes home McDonald's cross and confirming their first win of the campaign with a 30-yard sizzler from Lucas (who has signed a new contract), the O's rarely threaten up front. The supply lines to the forwards are the weakest point.

4. A poor match springs into life with O'Brien's goal and Orient only stay in contention with a couple of fine saves from George. Then out of nothing Foster cracks an equaliser and suddenly McDonald lets rip from distance to gain revenge for last week.

5. Carey has finally got his team playing the way he wants and the result is Orient's biggest away league win since 1954. Hero of the day is Graham who has finally signed a new contract and celebrates with a clinically-taken hat-trick. It's Walsall's first home defeat in 17 months.

6. The scoreline is tough on Derby who dominate the first half, but the prizes go to the team that can score. Swallow toe-punts the ball into his own net as he intercepts Dunmore's pass, followed by a penalty after Conwell uses his hands to deny McDonald. The win puts Orient second.

7. Rovers had lost every game up till now, but they chalk up a win against a side who over-elaborate on the ball. George's goal takes on the appearance of a shooting gallery before Hooper finally opens the scoring and Jones nabs the second. Graham is brought down for the penalty.

8. Orient finally turn it on for their home fans and the much-fancied Terriers are terrorised. Their goal is under almost constant pressure and England's left-back Ray Wilson makes two mistakes that result in goals. Coddington pulls a muscle early on and plays as a makeshift striker.

9. Once-mighty Preston are a pale shadow of the great fifties side and their fans' feelings can be gauged by the crowd figure – a fraction of the gates they used to get. They gain their first home win since March, but nearly throw it away as the visitors come back strongly and nearly level.

10. Town's centre-half Bob Parker is carried off with a dislocated shoulder, quickly followed by them conceding a goal. A brawl develops in the second half, resulting in a booking for McDonald and a coin-pelting for keeper George. Dunmore hits a post and it proves costly at the death.

#		Date	Att	Pos				Res	HT
11	H PLYMOUTH	29/9	13,398	4	L	7	12	1:2	0-2

Dunmore 89 / Williams K 1, 41 — Ref: K Collinge

George	Charlton	Lewis	Lucas	Bishop	Lea	White	Foster	Dunmore	Graham	McDonald
MacLaren	Robertson	Fulton	Williams JS	Fincham	Newman	Anderson	Williams K	Jackson	McAnearney	Malloy

Keith Williams shocks Orient inside a minute and this emergency inside-right is the man-of-the-match. Orient only start to play well in the second half, but Dunmore misses a one-on-one with the keeper before his late consolation. Is Carey going to have to change his side soon?

12	H STOKE	7/10	10,621	3	W	19	14	3-0	3-0

Foster 3, Graham 33, Dunmore 38 — Ref: P Rose

George	Charlton	Lewis	Lucas	Bishop	Lea	White	Foster	Dunmore	Graham	McDonald
O'Neill	Asprey	Allen	Howitt	Andrew	Skeels	Ratcliffe	Mudie	Bullock	Thompson	Adam

Carey names an unchanged line-up for the twelfth successive league game and they roast an abysmal Stoke side in the first half. Foster taps in the early opener and Graham makes it two with an angled drive. Dunmore takes the ball out of the keeper's hands for the killer third goal.

13	A SUNDERLAND	14/10	36,780	5	L	8	14	1:2	1-1

Dunmore 10 / Clough 26, 51 — Ref: J Kelly

George	Charlton	Lewis	Lucas	Bishop	Lea	White	Foster	Dunmore	Graham	McDonald
Wakeham	Irwin	Ashurst	Anderson	Hurley	McNab	Hooper	Herd	Clough	Gibbs	Dillon

Orient outplay Sunderland for much of the game and the tenth-minute opener is their fourth goal attempt (three were missed by Gibbs, Carey's first change of the season). The O's are undone by scoring sensation Brian Clough who lets fly with a couple of shots that are too hot to handle.

14	H ROTHERHAM	21/10	10,581	6	D	5	15	0-0	1-1

Graham 49 / Perry 80p — Ref: E Norman

George	Charlton	Lewis	Lucas	Bishop	Lea	White	Foster	Dunmore	Graham	McDonald
Morritt	Perry	Morgan	Lambert	Lancaster	Cassidy	Wilson	Weston	Houghton	Kirkman	Taylor

Foster's performance attracts the interest of England manager Walter Winterbottom who dispatches Billy Wright to report on him. He should have chosen an away game, because the O's are mediocre at Brisbane Road this year. A win is denied by Lea's foul on Cassidy in the box.

15	A LIVERPOOL	28/10	36,612	7	D	1	16	2-1	3-3

Dunmore 26, 75, Foster 35 / Hunt 34, 50, Leishman 79 — Ref: V James

George	Charlton	Lewis	Lucas	Bishop	Lea	White	Foster	Dunmore	Graham	McDonald
Slater	White	Byrne	Milne	Yeats	Leishman	Lewis	Hunt	St John	Melia	A'Court

Orient earn the respect of the Kop by taking the lead three times against Bill Shankly's rejuvenated Liverpool. Dunmore's goals consist of a 40-yard screamer and a beautiful header. Hunt's second equalising header embarrassingly drops out of George's hands and trickles into the net.

16	H CHARLTON	4/11	13,120	7	W	22	18	2-1	0-0

Dunmore 47, 68p, Lawrie 88 — Ref: F Cowen

George	Charlton	Lewis	Lucas	Bishop	Lea	White	Foster	Dunmore	Graham	McDonald
Duff	Sewell	Hewie	Tocknell	Hinton	Bailey	Lawrie	Matthews	Edwards	Leary	Kinsey

A hefty gate inside Brisbane Road witnesses another mediocre home display. Dunmore continues his hot form by stealing a goal after Duff and Sewell get themselves into a muddle. He adds another when Sewell handles, but the Valiants come back and nearly equalise right at the death.

17	A LEEDS	11/11	7,967	6	D	21	19	0-0	0-0

Ref: W Robinson

George	Charlton	Lewis	Lucas	Bishop	Lea	White	Elwood	Dunmore	Graham	McDonald
Younger	Hair	Bell	Smith	Goodwin	McConnell	Mayers	Bremner	Revie	Peyton	Hawksby

Elwood gets a rare start in place of the injured Foster, but he can't inspire his side into beating the hapless Leeds who are staring relegation to the Third in the face. Dunmore hits a post and Graham misses a good chance with a shot on his weaker right foot. O's should have won this.

18	H BRIGHTON	18/11	10,395	4	W	15	21	4-1	4-0

Dunm're 15, Elwood 25, Sitford 37 (og), [White 44], Nicholas 82 — Ref: K Seddon

George	Charlton	Lewis	Lucas	Bishop	Lea	White	Foster	Dunmore	Graham	McDonald
Baker	McNicol	Sitford	Bertolini	Jennings	Burtenshaw	Tiddy	Nicholas	Brown	Goodchild	Laverick

Promotion seems a possibility as Brighton are thrashed in a peerless first-half display. Elwood gets the goal of the game with a top-spin drive that dips over Baker's head and under the bar. Albion improve in the second half and Nicholas pulls one back. Carey may be signing him.

19	A SCUNTHORPE	24/11	11,712	2	W	3	23	1-0	2-0

McDonald 11, White 90 — Ref: K Howley

George	Charlton	Lewis	Lucas	Bishop	Lea	White	Foster	Dunmore	Graham	McDonald
Jones	Horstead	Brownsword	Gibson	Neale	Howells	Marriott	Kaye	Thomas	Godfrey	Wilson

In a classic smash-and-grab raid, Orient plunder an early goal through the unmarked McDonald, then defend in depth. Scunthorpe's normally prolific attack is stifled and their first home defeat is confirmed when White's drive spins over the goalie's head. Orient are now in second.

20	H NORWICH	2/12	12,908	2	W	11	25	1-0	2-0

Dunmore 27, 75 — Ref: J Cooke

George	Charlton	Lewis	Lucas	Bishop	Lea	White	Foster	Dunmore	Graham	McDonald
Barnsley	McCrohan	Ashman	Scott	Butler	Crowe	Waites	Allcock	Conway	Hill	Punton

Dunmore turns in one of his best-ever displays for Orient to impress the watching Cliff Richard. He floats a free-kick over the combined City defence and then beats three defenders before cracking in a fine second. Barnsley, despite being injured, keeps the score down with fine saves.

21	H NEWCASTLE	16/12	13,261	2	W	14	27	2-0	1-0

White 31, Elwood 57 — Ref: P Tuck

George	Charlton	Lewis	Lucas	Bishop	Lea	White	Foster	Dunmore	Graham	McDonald
Robertson	McKinney	McMichael	Wright	McGrath	Bell	Hughes	Allchurch	White	Elwood	Wilson J
Hollins									McGuigan	

Once more the granite defence holds firm to deny the opposition whilst the forwards do just enough to earn the win. White sneaks in a header and Elwood adds a second as the Magpies defence waits in vain for the referee to blow up for a foul. Robertson makes two world-class saves.

LEAGUE DIVISION 2   Manager: Johnny Carey   SEASON 1961-62

No	Date		Opponent	Att	Pos	Pt	F-A	H-T	Scorers, Times, and Referees	1	2	3	4	5	6	7	8	9	10	11
22	23/12	A	MIDDLESBROUGH	9,955	19	29	3-2	2-1	Dunmore 11, Foster 43, 47 / Harris 27p, 66p / Ref: A Atterton	George *Appleby*	Charlton *Stonehouse*	Lewis *McNeil*	Lucas *Yeoman*	Bishop *Thomson*	Lea *Neal*	White *Day*	Foster *Kaye*	Dunmore *Peacock*	Elwood *Harris*	McDonald *Holliday*
23	26/12	H	SWANSEA	14,550	15	31	1-0	1-0	Dunmore 30 / Ref: A Moore	George *King*	Charlton *Sanders*	Lewis *Griffiths*	Lucas *Davies P*	Bishop *Nurse*	Lea *Williams H*	White *Jones*	Foster *Davies R*	Dunmore *Webster*	Elwood *Donnelly*	McDonald *Williams G*
24	30/12	A	SWANSEA	9,000	15	33	3-1	1-1	Dunmore 11, 64, 76 / Donnelly 31 / Ref: W Clements	George *Dwyer*	Charlton *Sanders*	Lewis *Griffiths*	Lucas *Davies P*	Bishop *Nurse*	Lea *Williams H*	White *Jones*	Foster *Davies R*	Dunmore *Reynolds*	Elwood *Donnelly*	McDonald *Williams G*
25	13/1	H	WALSALL	15,113	13	35	3-0	0-0	Dunmore 61p, Graham 64, White 79 / Ref: R Smith	George *Boswell*	Charlton *Sharples*	Lewis *Guttridge*	Lucas *Hill*	Bishop *McPherson*	Lea *Dudley*	White *Meek*	Foster *Hodgkisson*	Dunmore *Beaman*	Graham *Foster*	Newman *Taylor*
26	20/1	A	DERBY	22,136	5	37	2-1	0-1	Dunmore 65p, Graham 72 / Curry 17 / Ref: J Kelly	George *Matthews*	Charlton *Barrowcliffe*	Lewis *Davies*	Lucas *Parry*	Bishop *Moore*	Lea *Hopkinson*	White *Roby*	Foster *Havenhand*	Dunmore *Curry*	Graham *Swallow*	Newman *Palmer*
27	3/2	H	BRISTOL ROV	14,737	21	37	2-3	1-1	McDonald 25, Graham 60 / Williams 20, Mabbutt 48, Jarman 78 / Ref: G McCabe	George *Radford*	Charlton *Bradford*	Lewis *Frowen*	Lucas *Bumpstead*	Bishop *Pyle*	Lea *Sykes*	White *Jarman*	Foster *Williams*	Dunmore *Mabbutt*	Graham *Jones*	McDonald *Hooper*
28	9/2	H	PRESTON	18,899	10	37	0-2	0-1	Spavin 14, Smith 89 / Ref: H Horner	George *Kelly*	Charlton *Cunningham*	Lewis *Ross*	Lucas *Wylie*	Bishop *Singleton*	Lea *Smith*	White *Wilson D*	Foster *Biggs*	Dunmore *Alston*	Graham *Spavin*	McDonald *Thompson*
29	17/2	A	PLYMOUTH	20,531	3	37	1-2	0-2	Newman 22, McAnearney 36 / Ref: S Yates	Robertson *MacLaren*	Charlton *Robertson*	Lewis *Fulton*	Lucas *Williams JS*	Bishop *Fincham*	Lea *Newman*	White *Anderson*	Foster *Carter*	Dunmore *Kirby*	Graham *McAnearney*	Newman *Malloy*
30	24/2	A	STOKE	21,846	8	39	1-0	0-0	Dunmore 62 / Ref: A Luty	Robertson *O'Neill*	Wright *Asprey*	Lewis *Allen*	Lucas *Howitt*	Bishop *Andrew*	Lea *Skeels*	Deeley *Matthews*	Taylor *Thompson*	Dunmore *Nibloe*	Foster *Violet*	Elwood *Ratcliffe*
31	3/3	H	SUNDERLAND	19,974	7	40	1-1	0-1	Deeley 55 / McPheat 3 / Ref: F Stringer	Robertson *Montgomery*	Charlton *Irwin*	Lewis *Ashurst*	Lucas *Anderson*	Bishop *Rooks*	Lea *McNab*	Deeley *Davison*	Foster *Herd*	Dunmore *O'Neill J*	**Bolland** *McPheat*	Elwood *Overfield*

22 — Middlesbrough: Foster does his chances of selection for England's Youth team a power of good with a diving header and a neat shot to secure the points. A pair of penalties (the first given when Lewis's hand prevents a certain goal) flatters Boro, but Orient's attack is superior enough to justify the win.

23 — Swansea: The Welsh team can't unlock Orient's defence and so resort to rough-house tactics in frustration. The referee does little to stop the argy-bargy and the crowd complain bitterly, especially when he ignores a blatant handball in the area by Nurse. Dunmore converts from six yards to win it.

24 — Swansea: If Spurs had managed to sign Mel Charles three years ago, then Dunmore would have been given to Swansea in return. He shows them what they have been missing as he cracks in a hat-trick. Town actually have far more possession, but their attacks fail as the O's defence stands firm.

25 — Walsall: The O's strike the woodwork four times before a foul on Foster allows Dunmore to stroke his penalty wide of Boswell. Graham rapidly heads in the second goal, then Boswell manages to fumble White's cross into his own net. Casual supporters are now coming back to Brisbane Road.

26 — Derby: It's blood and guts which are on display more than skill as the fouls come thick and fast. Moore fouls Dunmore, but the O's striker is booked for gaining revenge on him. Dunmore has the last laugh by converting a penalty (Parry handball) and neatly creating the winner for Graham.

27 — Bristol Rov: Orient's nine-match winning run is brought to a halt as they succumb to their bogey team. For once the defence is deficient as Rovers strike three times. Williams opens the scoring with a 30-yarder on his club debut. Jarman silences 14,000 Orient supporters with his winning goal.

28 — Preston: Friday night games bring bumper crowds to Brisbane Road as Spurs and Hammers fans (amongst others) pay their respects. They witness a tired O's side suffering their third home defeat in six days. England manager Walter Winterbottom casts his eyes on Dunmore, who plays well.

29 — Plymouth: Argyle close the gap on Orient as the February blues continue. The Devon side admit they are lucky to win as they are generally outplayed, but they are far more clinical finishers. Deeley – Orient's new signing from Wolves – is one of the guilty players who miss good chances to score.

30 — Stoke: Stan Matthews (46) is the man who has sparked City back to life since his return to Stoke in October. Their seven-match winning home run is curtailed when Dunmore smacks in another long-distance effort. Even the genius of Matthews struggles against Orient's masterful defence.

31 — Sunderland: The O's sign 18-year-old Bolland from Chelsea for £4,500 just three hours before kick-off as they try to relieve the overworked Dunmore. He hits the crossbar, but Deeley is the hero as he floats in a cross that hoodwinks Montgomery. McPheat had chested in the early opening goal.

Match results

#	H/A	Opponent	Date	Div	Res	Pts	HT	FT	Opp Pos	Att
32	A	ROTHERHAM	9/3	2	L	40	0-1	1-2	5	10,697
33	A	BURY	13/3	2	W	42	1-0	1-0	16	9,592
34	H	LIVERPOOL	17/3	2	D	43	1-0	2-2	1	25,880
35	A	CHARLTON	24/3	2	W	45	2-1	2-1	22	29,298
36	H	LEEDS	31/3	2	D	46	0-0	0-0	21	13,290
37	A	BRIGHTON	7/4	2	W	48	1-0	1-0	22	12,927
38	H	SCUNTHORPE	14/4	2	L	48	0-1	0-1	4	16,867
39	H	LUTON	20/4	2	D	49	0-0	0-0	13	21,292
40	A	NORWICH	21/4	2	D	50	0-0	0-0	17	20,454
41	A	LUTON	23/4	2	W	52	1-1	3-1	15	13,681
42	H	BURY	28/4	2	W	54	1-0	2-0	18	21,617

Home 14,787
Away 17,572
Average 17,572

---

32 — A ROTHERHAM, 9/3 (0-1)
Scorers: Lucas 77 — *Weston 32, Houghton 70*. Ref: H Richards
O's: Robertson, Charlton, Lewis, Lucas, Bishop, Lea, White, Taylor, Dunmore, Bolland, Deeley
Rotherham: *Ironside, Jackson, Morgan, Cassidy, Madden, Waterhouse, Kirkman, Weston, Houghton, Butler, Bambridge*

Orient have failed to win any in of their five visits to Millmoor and that run is extended by this defeat. Weston makes up for hitting a post by giving Town the lead and Houghton nets from a corner. Lucas narrows the gap from distance and Deeley hits the post with a last-minute shot.

33 — A BURY, 13/3 (1-0)
Scorers: McDonald 22. Ref: J Powell
O's: Robertson, Charlton, Lewis, Lucas, Bishop, Lea, Deeley, Bolland, Dunmore, Graham, McDonald
Bury: *Harker, Gallagher, Eastham, Turner, Stokoe, May, Calder, beaumont, Hickson, Jackson, Hubbard*

McDonald gets the winner by rapping one in from 30 yards as his colleagues shut up shop to keep the two points. Hickson does put the ball in the net for the home side but it is disallowed for a push on Bishop. The O's will need to be sharper for the visit of the mighty Liverpool.

34 — H LIVERPOOL, 17/3 (2-2)
Scorers: Graham 45, Lewis 83 — *A'Court 81, 89*. Ref: H Webb
O's: Robertson, Charlton, Lewis, Lucas, Bishop, Lea, Deeley, Taylor, Bolland, Graham, McDonald
Liverpool: *Furnell, Byrne, Moran, Milne, Yeats, Leishman, Callaghan, Hunt, St John, Melia, A'Court*

The O's defence keep the fearsome Hunt/St John partnership quiet. Yeats has an easier task in the absence of the injured Dunmore, but he is stunned when Graham glides past him and fires home. Hot-shot A'Court saves Pool twice, either side of Lewis's stinging 30-yard free-kick.

35 — A CHARLTON, 24/3 (2-1)
Scorers: Deeley 20, Graham 26 — *Kinsey 35*. Ref: G Pullin
O's: Robertson, Charlton, Lewis, Lucas, Bishop, Lea, Deeley, Bolland, Dunmore, Graham, McDonald
Charlton: *Duff, Sewell, Ord, Hewie, Hinton, Bailey, Lawrie, Matthews, Leary, Edwards, Kinsey*

Graham's dizzy run through their defence for the second goal would seem to ensure a comfortable victory for the O's, but they make heavy work of their win, not helped by an injury to Dunmore. A clash between Lea and Hewie nearly results in a mass brawl, till the ref steps in.

36 — H LEEDS, 31/3 (0-0)
Ref: H New
O's: Robertson, Charlton, Lewis, Lucas, Bishop, Lea, Deeley, Taylor, Bolland, Graham, McDonald
Leeds: *Younger, Hair, Mason, Goodwin, Charlton, Smith, Bremner, Collins, Lawson, Payton, Hawksby*

Another bore draw against a dour Leeds side that Don Revie is going to have to inspire if they are to avoid the drop into the Third. Orient aren't any better. Their injury-ravaged side don't appear to be able to penetrate a box of chocolates on this showing. The crowd slumbers.

37 — A BRIGHTON, 7/4 (1-0)
Scorers: Foster 20. Ref: J Finney
O's: Robertson, Charlton, Clark, Lucas, Bishop, Lea, Deeley, Foster, Bolland, Graham, McDonald
Brighton: *Baker, Carolan, Baxter, Bertolini, Jennings, Burtenshaw, Tiddy, Nicholas, Caven, McNeill, Laverick*

David Clark, the ex-Leyton centre-half, makes his debut at left-back as the O's injury woes increase. The visitors grind out an unconvincing win when Foster volleys in the winner. Referee Finney upsets the Goldstone Ground faithful by ruling that a Caven shot doesn't cross the line.

38 — H SCUNTHORPE, 14/4 (0-1)
Scorers: *Kaye 1*. Ref: G Roper
O's: Robertson, Charlton, Lewis, Lucas, Bishop, Lea, Deeley, Foster, Dunmore, Graham, McDonald
Scunthorpe: *Jones, John, Brownsword, Gibson, Neale, Howells, Marriott, Godfrey, Kaye, McGuigan, Wilson*

From the kick-off Lucas receives the ball then changes his mind about who he will pass to. It ends up going to a grateful McGuigan who tees up Kaye for the winner which is timed at nine seconds. An unfit Dunmore returns and the O's are toothless. Thankfully Plymouth lose as well.

39 — H LUTON, 20/4 (0-0)
Ref: J Loynton
O's: Robertson, Charlton, Lewis, Lucas, Bishop, Lea, Deeley, Taylor, Dunmore, Graham, McDonald
Luton: *Standen, McNally, Bramwell, Morton, Kelly, Pacey, Clarke, Turner, Ashworth, McKechnie, Fleming*

McDonald breezes through the Hatters' defence and fires home the winning goal. But how come it's a goalless draw? The answer is Dunmore who dives towards the goal, but who is offside. The referee gets bombarded with orange peel. The O's haven't won in seven at home now.

40 — A NORWICH, 21/4 (0-0)
Ref: R Leafe
O's: Robertson, Charlton, Lewis, Lucas, Bishop, Lea, Deeley, Taylor, Dunmore, Bolland, McDonald
Norwich: *Kennon, Thurlow, Ashman, Burton, Butler, Mullett, Mannion, Lythgoe, Scott, Hill, Punton*

Carey brings in Bolland but the goal drought continues. Norwich are just as bad at finishing, although they outplay the O's. The only time the visitors threaten to score is when Kennon completely misses a tame Dunmore shot. Ashman saves his blushes with a goal-line clearance.

41 — A LUTON, 23/4 (3-1)
Scorers: Gibbs 30, 55, Lucas 77 — *Morton 8*. Ref: L James
O's: Robertson, Charlton, Lewis, Lucas, Bishop, Lea, Deeley, Gibbs, Dunmore, Foster, McDonald
Luton: *Standen, McNally, Bramwell, Morton, Kelly, Pacey, Clarke, Ashworth, Baynham, McKechnie, Fleming*

When Dunmore has a penalty saved after Morton gives the Hatters an early lead, the visiting Orient fans fear the First Division may slip away from them. Then up steps Gibbs who dispatches a couple of goals to steer his side towards the promised land. Promotion is very close now.

42 — H BURY, 28/4 (2-0)
Scorers: Graham 14, 84. Ref: C Kingston
O's: Robertson, Charlton, Lewis, Lucas, Bishop, Lea, Deeley, Gibbs, Dunmore, Graham, McDonald
Bury: *Harker, Gallagher, Eastham, Turner, Stokoe, Atherton, Leech, Beaumont, Calder, Jackson, Hartley*

Player-manager Bob Stokoe, who will one day take Sunderland to the FA Cup, helps to keep the Rokerites out of the top flight when he is robbed by Graham on the touchline. He cuts in and nets from 15 yards for his second goal. Promotion is confirmed amidst joyous scenes.

LEAGUE DIVISION 2 (CUP-TIES) — Manager: Johnny Carey — SEASON 1961-62

League Cup

1 A STOCKPORT 11/9 — 7,615 4:20 — 2 W 1-0 H-T 1-0 — McDonald 23 — Ref: V James

1	2	3	4	5	6	7	8	9	10	11
George	Charlton	Lewis	Lucas	Bishop	Lea	White	Elwood	Dunmore	Graham	McDonald
Lea	*Murray*	*Webb*	*Birch*	*Hodder*	*Porteous*	*Ward*	*McDonnell*	*Anderson*	*Murdoch*	*Partridge*

McDonald grabs the winner from 25 yards after his initial shot is blocked by Porteous's legs. County come back strongly and twice Charlton is forced to clear balls off his line after George is beaten, but in the second half Orient let their superiority show. They're still unbeaten away.

2 H BLACKPOOL 4/10 — 9,910 1:17 — 4 D 1-1 H-T 0-0 — Gibbs 60 / *Oates 46* — Ref: K Collinge

1	2	3	4	5	6	7	8	9	10	11
George	Charlton	Lewis	Lucas	Bishop	Lea	White	Elwood	Gibbs	Graham	McDonald
West	*Armfield*	*Martin*	*Hauser*	*Gratrix*	*Durie*	*Horne*	*Peterson*	*Charnley*	*Parry*	*Oates*

The O's dominate top-flight Blackpool, but are left to rue their profligate finishing. They fall behind when a gentle cross finds its way into the net as three Orient defenders slip on the greasy surface. Gibb's earns a replay with a stinging shot that keeper West punches into his own net.

2R A BLACKPOOL 30/10 — 6,098 1:14 — 7 L 1-5 H-T 0-2 — McDonald 86 / *Parry 5, 11, Charnley 51, 73, 80* — Ref: R Harper

1	2	3	4	5	6	7	8	9	10	11
George	Charlton	Lewis	Lucas	Bishop	Lea	White	Elwood	Dunmore	Newman	McDonald
Waters	*Thompson*	*Martin*	*Crawford*	*Gratrix*	*Durie*	*Hill*	*Peterson*	*Charnley*	*Parry*	*Horne*

Two days after holding Liverpool at Anfield, Orient come a cropper at Bloomfield Road. Parry punishes them twice in the first half whilst Charnley runs riot after the break. It's an unhappy return to the side for Ron Newman who plays at inside-left in place of the injured Graham.

FA Cup

3 A BRENTFORD 6/1 — 19,700 3:23 — 2 D 1-1 H-T 0-1 — Foster 60 / *Summers 45* — Ref: C Kineston

1	2	3	4	5	6	7	8	9	10	11
George	Charlton	Lewis	Lucas	Bishop	Lea	White	Foster	Dunmore	Elwood	McDonald
Cakebread	*Coote*	*Gisham*	*Belcher*	*Gelson*	*Higginson*	*Summers*	*Brooks*	*Francis*	*Edgley*	*McLeod*

Brentford may be awaiting the drop into the basement, but they deserve more than a replay as they end the match with only nine fit men. Centre-half Gelson spends the second half limping on the wing and Summers is also crocked. Foster's goal on the hour spares Orient's blushes.

3R H BRENTFORD 8/1 — 22,690 3:23 — 2 W 2-1 H-T 0-1 — Foster 60, Elwood 85 / *Higginson 26* — Ref: C Kineston

1	2	3	4	5	6	7	8	9	10	11
George	Charlton	Lewis	Lucas	Bishop	Lea	White	Foster	Dunmore	Elwood	McDonald
Cakebread	*Coote*	*Gisham*	*Belcher*	*Dargie*	*Higginson*	*Rainford*	*Brooks*	*Francis*	*Edgley*	*McLeod*

A gale-force wind aids the Bees in the first half, but Orient pummel their goal remorselessly in the second half. Foster once more gets a goal on the hour, but this time he's flat on his back when he deflects a Lucas shot into the net. Cakebread makes about a baker's dozen-worth of saves.

4 A BURNLEY 30/1 — 37,932 1:1 — 2 D 1-1 H-T 0-0 — Foster 56 / *Harris 83* — Ref: V Jones

1	2	3	4	5	6	7	8	9	10	11
George	Charlton	Lewis	Lucas	Bishop	Lea	White	Foster	Dunmore	Graham	McDonald
Blacklaw	*Angus*	*Elder*	*Adamson*	*Cummings*	*Miller*	*Connelly*	*McIlroy*	*Pointer*	*Robson*	*Harris*

The First Division pacesetters pepper Orient's goal, but the Londoners gamely hang on. They take a shock lead when Foster latches onto Graham's flick-on, but parity is restored when Harris bangs one in. 'I have rarely seen a team [Orient] fight so hard,' says Burnley's Adamson.

4R H BURNLEY 6/2 — 31,000 1:1 — 2 L 0-1 H-T 0-0 — *Miller 60* — Ref: V Jones

1	2	3	4	5	6	7	8	9	10	11
George	Charlton	Lewis	Lucas	Bishop	Lea	White	Foster	Dunmore	Graham	McDonald
Blacklaw	*Angus*	*Elder*	*Adamson*	*Cummings*	*Miller*	*Connelly*	*McIlroy*	*Pointer*	*Robson*	*Harris*

The tables are turned in the replay as Orient outplay their more illustrious opponents. A rare capacity crowd at Brisbane Road is treated to a showing that proves that the O's are worthy First Division material. Lewis nearly knocks himself out on the post as he tries to clear the winner.

		Home					Away					
	P	W	D	L	F	A	W	D	L	F	A	Pts
1 Liverpool	42	18	3	0	68	19	9	5	7	31	24	62
2 LEYTON O	42	11	5	5	34	17	11	5	5	35	23	54
3 Sunderland	42	17	3	1	60	16	5	6	10	25	34	53
4 Scunthorpe	42	14	4	3	52	26	6	3	11	34	45	49
5 Plymouth	42	12	4	5	45	30	7	4	10	30	45	46
6 Southampton	42	13	3	5	53	28	5	6	10	24	34	45
7 Huddersfield	42	11	5	5	39	22	5	7	9	28	37	44
8 Stoke	42	13	4	4	34	17	4	4	13	21	40	42
9 Rotherham	42	9	6	6	36	30	7	3	11	34	46	41
10 Preston	42	11	4	6	34	23	4	6	11	21	34	40
11 Newcastle	42	10	5	6	40	27	5	4	12	24	31	39
12 Middlesbro'	42	11	3	7	45	29	5	4	12	31	43	39
13 Luton	42	12	1	8	44	37	5	4	12	25	34	39
14 Walsall	42	11	7	3	42	23	3	4	14	28	52	39
15 Charlton	42	10	5	6	38	30	5	4	12	31	45	39
16 Derby	42	10	7	4	42	27	4	4	13	26	48	39
17 Norwich	42	10	6	5	36	28	4	5	12	25	42	39
18 Bury	42	9	4	8	32	36	8	1	12	20	40	39
19 Leeds	42	9	6	6	24	19	3	6	12	26	42	36
20 Swansea	42	10	5	6	38	30	2	7	12	23	53	36
21 Bristol Rov	42	11	3	7	36	31	2	4	15	17	50	33
22 Brighton	42	7	7	7	24	32	3	4	14	18	54	31
	924	249	100	113	896	577	113	100	249	577	896	924

Odds & ends

Double wins: (8) Brighton, Bury, Charlton, Derby, Middlesbrough, Stoke, Swansea, Walsall.
Double losses: (3) Bristol R, Plymouth, Preston.

Won from behind: (3) Southampton (a), Derby (a), Luton (a).
Lost from in front: (1) Sunderland (a).

High spots: Promotion to the top flight for the first time.
The attractive passing game that proved so successful.
The appointment of Carey as manager which led to the above.
Lucas, Bishop and Lea: the best half-back line in football.
Dave Dunmore: 22 goals for the season.

Low spots: An average home attendance of 14,787. In the 1956-57 promotion season the average was 17,254.
The stuttering attack: 69 goals is a low total for a promoted side.
Failing to take their chances to beat Blackpool in the FA Cup.

Hat-tricks: (2) Graham, Dunmore.
Ever-presents: (3) Bishop, Lea, Lucas.
Leading scorer: Dunmore (22).

	Appearances			Goals			
	Lge	LC	FAC	Lge	LC	FAC	Tot
Bishop, Sid	42	3	4				
Bolland, Gordon	8						
Charlton, Stan	41	3	4				
Clark, David	1						
Deeley, Norman	14		4	2			2
Dunmore, David	39	2	4	22			22
Elwood, Joe	10	3	2	2		1	3
Foster, Ron	33		4	10		3	13
George, Frank	26	3					
Gibbs, Derek	3	1					
Graham, Malcolm	29	2	2	2	1		3
Lea, Cyril	42	3	4	13			13
Lewis, Eddie	41	3	4	1			1
Lucas, Malcolm	42	3	4	3			3
McDonald, Terry	36	3	4	6	2		8
Newman, Ron	2	1					
Robertson, Willie	16						
Taylor, Willie	6						
White, Phil	30	3	4	6			6
Wright, George	1						
(own goals)				2			2
20 players used	462	33	44	69	3	4	76

LEAGUE DIVISION 1

Manager: Johnny Carey

SEASON 1962-63

Column legend for line-ups: 1–11 give the Orient player (roman) with the opposing player (italic) below.

---

1 — H ARSENAL — 18/8
Att 26,300 · Pos 16 *5* · L · Pt 0 · F-A 1-2 · H-T 0-1

1	2	3	4	5	6	7	8	9	10	11
Robertson	Charlton	Lewis	Lucas	Bishop	Lea	Deeley	Gibbs	Dunmore	Graham	McDonald
McKechnie	*Magill*	*McCullough*	*Brown*	*Neill*	*Snedden*	*Armstrong*	*Strong*	*Baker*	*Barnwell*	*Skirton*

Scorers: Gibbs 75 / *Strong 36, Baker 51* · Ref: G Pullin

The biggest home league gate in six years sees Orient denied a penalty when Neill seems to haul down Dunmore. Arsenal score a couple of pearlers to win the game, but Gibbs caps a fine game by scoring Orient's first goal in the top flight. He beats two defenders to a loose ball.

---

2 — A WEST BROM — 22/8
Att 22,409 · Pos 20 *7* · L · Pt 0 · F-A 1-2 · H-T 0-1

1	2	3	4	5	6	7	8	9	10	11
Robertson	Charlton	Lewis	Lucas	Bishop	Lea	Deeley	Gibbs	Dunmore	Graham	McDonald
Millington	*Howe*	*Williams G*	*Williams S*	*Jones*	*Drury*	*Jackson*	*Burnside*	*Smith*	*Kevan*	*Clark*

Scorers: Dunmore 86 / *Smith 40, Kevan 57* · Ref: J Cattlin

A dour game follows the template of the opener as the visitors take a two-goal lead. Clive Clark and Don Howe provide the crosses that are headed in. The O's will have to get points from mediocre opposition like this if they are to survive. The Baggies claim offside for the O's goal.

---

3 — A BIRMINGHAM — 25/8
Att 23,500 · Pos 18 *20* · D · Pt 1 · F-A 2-2 · H-T 2-1

1	2	3	4	5	6	7	8	9	10	11
Robertson	Charlton	Lewis	Lucas	Bishop	Lea	Deeley	Gibbs	Dunmore	Graham	McDonald
Schofield	*Lynn*	*Sissons*	*Hennessey*	*Smith*	*Beard*	*Hellawell*	*Bullock*	*Stubbs*	*Leek*	*Thwaites*

Scorers: Graham 22, Dunmore 41p / *Bullock 6, Hellawell 56* · Ref: J Bullough

The last thing that the O's need is to concede an early goal, but they show great heart by coming back strongly. Graham converts a Deeley cross and then Dunmore nets from the spot after Sissons handles. Hellawell prevents the first win when his cross hoodwinks goalie Robertson.

---

4 — H WEST BROM — 29/8
Att 17,289 · Pos 20 *9* · L · Pt 1 · F-A 2-3 · H-T 1-3

1	2	3	4	5	6	7	8	9	10	11
Robertson	Charlton	Lewis	Lucas	Bishop	Lea	Deeley	Gibbs	Dunmore	Graham	McDonald
Potter	*Howe*	*Williams G*	*Williams S*	*Jones*	*Drury*	*Jackson*	*Hope*	*Smith*	*Kevan*	*Clark*

Scorers: Deeley 23, Dunmore 72p / *Lewis 18 (og), Lea 37 (og), Clark 39* · Ref: K Howley

Orient dominate the match and win 19 corners, but a hat-trick of defensive errors prove fatal. Lewis's attempted clearance is misdirected and then he hesitates to allow Jackson's piledriver, which Lea deflects into the net. Kevan barges Robertson which allows Clark an easy goal.

---

5 — H WEST HAM — 1/9
Att 23,918 · Pos 18 *22* · W · Pt 3 · F-A 2-0 · H-T 2-0

1	2	3	4	5	6	7	8	9	10	11
Robertson	Charlton	Lewis	Lucas	Bishop	Lea	Deeley	Bolland	Dunmore	Graham	McDonald
Leslie	*Kirkup*	*Burkett*	*Peters*	*Brown*	*Moore*	*Dear*	*Woosnam*	*Sealey*	*Byrne*	*Crawford*

Scorers: Dunmore 5, Graham 40 / · Ref: J Pickles

Bobby Moore signs a new contract just before the kick-off to end a pay dispute. He doesn't get a win bonus today though. Dunmore nods home an early corner, but Graham's goal is sensational. He runs 40 yards, leaving defenders in his wake, pauses, and then cracks in a 25-yard corker.

---

6 — A EVERTON — 5/9
Att 51,542 · Pos 19 *1* · L · Pt 3 · F-A 0-3 · H-T 0-2

1	2	3	4	5	6	7	8	9	10	11
Robertson	Charlton	Lewis	Lucas	Bishop	Lea	Deeley	Bolland	Dunmore	Graham	McDonald
West	*Meagan*	*Thomson*	*Gabriel*	*Labone*	*Harris*	*Bingham*	*Stevens*	*Young*	*Vernon*	*Morrissey*

Scorers: / *Bingham 4, Gabriel 44, Vernon 58p* · Ref: J Taylor

O's manager Johnny Carey assembled most of Everton's side when he was their boss, and their clinical, professional performance can be seen as a backhanded compliment to him. Orient play pretty football, but only a world-class collection of saves from Robertson prevents a rout.

---

7 — H MANCHESTER U — 8/9
Att 24,901 · Pos 18 *17* · W · Pt 5 · F-A 1-0 · H-T 0-0

1	2	3	4	5	6	7	8	9	10	11
Robertson	Charlton	Lewis	Lucas	Bishop	Lea	Deeley	Bolland	Dunmore	Graham	McDonald
Gaskell	*Brennan*	*Dunne*	*Nicholson*	*Foulkes*	*Lawton*	*Moir*	*Setters*	*Herd*	*Law*	*McMillan*

Scorers: McDonald 89 / · Ref: J Osborne

Matt Busby has signed Denis Law from Torino for £115,000, but the huge number of casual fans who have come to gawp at him are left to admire Orient's strikers instead. Gaskell pulls off a non-stop array of master saves, but finally succumbs to McDonald's sweet chip at the end.

---

8 — H EVERTON — 12/9
Att 21,756 · Pos 13 *2* · W · Pt 7 · F-A 3-0 · H-T 0-0

1	2	3	4	5	6	7	8	9	10	11
Robertson	Charlton	Lewis	Lucas	Bishop	Lea	Deeley	Bolland	Dunmore	Graham	McDonald
West	*Meagan*	*Thomson*	*Sharples*	*Labone*	*Harris*	*Bingham*	*Stevens*	*Young*	*Vernon*	*Morrissey*

Scorers: Deeley 53, Bolland 57, Dunmore 78 / · Ref: T Dawes

Last week's scoreline is reversed, as McDonald inspires his fellow men to what is their greatest-ever victory. The League-leaders are knocked off the top by a Deeley shot from a Lucas pass, and two superlative crosses from McDonald. Robertson is unbeatable and Carey is ecstatic.

---

9 — A BURNLEY — 15/9
Att 24,978 · Pos 16 *8* · L · Pt 7 · F-A 0-2 · H-T 0-1

1	2	3	4	5	6	7	8	9	10	11
Robertson	Charlton	Lewis	Lucas	Bishop	Lea	Deeley	Bolland	Dunmore	Graham	McDonald
Blacklaw	*Angus*	*Elder*	*Walker*	*Talbut*	*Miller*	*Connelly*	*Pointer*	*Lochhead*	*McIlroy*	*Harris*

Scorers: / *McIlroy 43, Lochhead 57* · Ref: J Carr

Burnley have made an uncharacteristically poor start to the season, and their new-look three man attack peppers the resolute Orient defence mercilessly, which succumbs twice, despite Robertson's brilliance in goal. The O's attack is energetic and willing, but sadly toothless today.

---

10 — H SHEFFIELD WED — 22/9
Att 20,125 · Pos 17 *9* · L · Pt 7 · F-A 2-4 · H-T 1-2

1	2	3	4	5	6	7	8	9	10	11
Robertson	Charlton	Lewis	Lucas	Bishop	Lea	Deeley	Bolland	Dunmore	Graham	McDonald
Springett	*Johnson*	*Megson*	*Eustace*	*Swan*	*Kaye*	*Wilkinson*	*Quinn*	*Layne*	*Dobson*	*Holliday*

Scorers: Bolland 42, Deeley 55 / *Layne 16, Dobson 34, Kaye 64, [Quinn 82]* · Ref: N Matthews

A bad-tempered game in which Bronco Layne is booked and several players square up to each other and exchange the odd sly punch, but it's the Owls who are the big hitters in front of goal. An angry mob of O's fans invade the pitch at the end and surround Layne and captain Kay.

11	A	FULHAM	12	W	2-0	2-0	Graham 30, McDonald 44	Robertson	Charlton	Lewis	Lucas	Clark	Lea	Deeley	Bolland	Dunmore	Graham	McDonald
	29/9	*26,505*	*21*	9				*Macedo*	*Keetch*	*Langley*	*Mullery*	*Dodgin*	*Robson*	*Key*	*Cook*	*Brown S*	*Henderson*	*Chamberlain*
							Ref: F Cowen	Fulham dominate the possession, but without the inspiration of the injured Johnny Haynes, fail to punish the sturdy defence of the visitors, for whom David Clark has a wonderful game as a replacement for the crocked Bishop. Both Orient goals result from blunders by keeper Macedo.										
12	A	MANCHESTER C	14	L	0-2	0-0		Robertson	Charlton	Lewis	Lucas	Clark	Lea	Deeley	Bolland	Dunmore	Graham	McDonald
	6/10	*19,706*	*16*	9			*Hannah 73, Harley 81*	*Dowd*	*Betts*	*Sear*	*Kennedy*	*Leivers*	*Benson*	*Young*	*Dobing*	*Harley*	*Hannah*	*Wagstaffe*
							Ref: T Reynolds	In a complete contrast to the last League game, Orient have the majority of the play but once more draw a complete blank, despite playing the team who will end up with the worst defensive record in the division. Deeley is criticised the most today as the Citizens score two late goals.										
13	H	BLACKPOOL	19	L	0-2	0-2		Robertson	Charlton	Lewis	Lucas	Clark	Lea	Deeley	Waites	Dunmore	Graham	McDonald
	13/10	17,156	*12*	9			*Parry 2, 16*	*Waiters*	*Armfield*	*Martin*	*Crawford*	*Gratrix*	*Durie*	*Watt*	*McPhee*	*Charnley*	*Parry*	*Horne*
							Ref: S Yates	Ray Parry takes his goalscoring chances with aplomb, unlike the Orientals who all fire blanks. Tangerine boss Ronnie Suart says 'Orient were unlucky not to get one goal, and if they had got one I fear they'd have got another.' The defeat drops the home side back towards the bottom.										
14	A	ASTON VILLA	19	L	0-1	0-0		Robertson	Charlton	Taylor	Gibbs	Bishop	Lea	Waites	Bolland	Dunmore	Graham	Deeley
	20/10	*29,370*	*6*	9			*Burrows 77*	*Sims*	*Neal*	*Aitken*	*Lee*	*Sleeuwenh'k*	*Tindall*	*Ewing*	*Wylie*	*Thomson*	*O'Neill*	*Burrows*
							Ref: C Duxbury	Orient (Lucas) and Villa (Dougan and Deakin) have key players, who are away on international duty. Villa feature six reserves, but they are still too good for the O's, who have a penalty appeal turned down just before the break when Aitken handles. A mis-hit cross provides the goal.										
15	H	TOTTENHAM	22	L	1-5	1-3	Deeley 26 *[White 63, Jones 85]*	**Pinner**	Charlton	Taylor	Lucas	Bishop	Lea	Deeley	Bolland	Dunmore	Foster	McDonald
	27/10	30,987	*1*	9			*White 21, Bishop 35 (og), Medwin 44,*	*Brown*	*Baker*	*Henry*	*Blanchflower*	*Norman*	*Marchi*	*Medwin*	*White*	*Allen*	*Greaves*	*Jones*
							Ref: D Smith	Brisbane Road enjoys a 30,000 crowd for a league match for the first time in its 25-year Orient history, though it's someway short of the 37,615 that saw this fixture at Millfields Road in 1929. Top-of-the-table Spurs are rampant and no side could have survived the onslaught.										
16	A	NOTT'M FOREST	22	D	1-1	0-1	Dunmore 50	Pinner	Charlton	Taylor	Lucas	Bishop	Lea	Deeley	Bolland	Dunmore	Foster	McDonald
	3/11	*17,821*	*6*	10			*Quigley 39*	*Armstrong*	*Wilson*	*Gray*	*Whitefoot*	*McKinlay*	*Winfield*	*Hockey*	*Quigley*	*Julians*	*Palmer*	*Le Flem*
							Ref: A Luty	After Le Flem's cross catches him unawares for the Forest goal, Pinner is able to settle down and enjoy his game without the fear of another thrashing. Foster also has more space and possession to show his worth at inside-left. Dunmore ends his goal drought to save a valuable point.										
17	H	IPSWICH	22	L	1-2	1-2	Gregory 14	Pinner	Charlton	Taylor	Lucas	Bishop	Lea	Deeley	**Gregory**	Dunmore	Foster	McDonald
	10/11	13,929	*20*	10			*Blackwood 30, Baxter 32*	*Bailey*	*Carberry*	*Malcolm*	*Baxter*	*Nelson*	*Pickett*	*Stephenson*	*Moran*	*Crawford*	*Blackwood*	*Leadbetter*
							Ref: H New	Gregory makes a wonderful start to his O's career by giving his side the lead. Ipswich are the league champions, but they appear to be one-season wonders. Two quick goals save them from the ignominy of replacing Orient at the bottom, but Dunmore has a penalty saved soon after.										
18	A	LIVERPOOL	22	L	0-5	0-3	*[St John 64]*	George	Charlton	Taylor	Lucas	Bishop	Lea	Deeley	Gregory	Dunmore	Foster	McDonald
	17/11	*30,009*	*10*	10			*Hunt 9, 24, 59, Stevenson 34,*	*Lawrence*	*Byrne*	*Moran*	*Milne*	*Yeats*	*Stevenson*	*Callaghan*	*Hunt*	*St John*	*Melia*	*A'Court*
							Ref: K Tuck	Rain, sleet, snow and wind combine to make life as difficult as possible for the players, but Liverpool's attack overcomes this to go nap. It's not as if Orient don't have the chances to match Pool, but the difference in quality of the two attacks is all too starkly displayed for all to see.										
19	H	WOLVERHAMPTON	22	L	0-4	0-2		George	Charlton	Lewis	Gibbs	Bishop	Lea	Dunmore	Taylor	Gregory	Lucas	Deeley
	24/11	16,431	*6*	10			*Hinton 12, Crowe 44, Stobart 56, 73*	*Davies*	*Showell*	*Thomson*	*Kirkham*	*Slater*	*Flowers*	*Wharton*	*Crowe*	*Stobart*	*Broadbent*	*Hinton*
							Ref: K Tuck	Brisbane Road now has a thick carpet of mud down the centre of the pitch, but the visitors don't seem hindered by this as they roast the O's, who are literally bogged down by their lack of width. Orient's poor attack makes it easy for the top sides to overrun their overworked defence.										
20	A	BLACKBURN	22	D	1-1	0-1	Graham 71	Pinner	Charlton	Lewis	Lucas	Bishop	Lea	Deeley	Gregory	Dunmore	Graham	McDonald
	1/12	*15,500*	*9*	11			*Harrison 33*	*Else*	*Bray*	*Newton*	*Clayton*	*Woods*	*McGrath*	*Haverty*	*Ferguson*	*Pickering*	*Douglas*	*Harrison*
							Ref: W Clements	Johnny Carey was Blackburn's boss from 1953 to 1958, so he knows how to stop them. He makes sure England international outside-right Bryan Douglas is marked out of the game, so that only leaves nine more outfield players to take care of. Graham earns a point on his return.										
21	H	SHEFFIELD UTD	22	D	2-2	1-1	Graham 4, Dunmore 78	Pinner	Charlton	Lewis	Gibbs	Bishop	Lea	Deeley	Taylor	Dunmore	Graham	McDonald
	8/12	9,874	*11*	12			*Shaw G 30p, Pace 58*	*Hodgkinson*	*Coldwell*	*Shaw G*	*Richardson*	*Shaw J*	*Summers*	*Allchurch*	*Kettleborough*	*Pace*	*Hodgson*	*Simpson*
							Ref: A Moore	Graham runs half the length of the pitch leaving defenders trailing in his wake, before despatching a trademark rocket shot. Lea is then controversially adjudged to have fouled Kettleborough for the penalty, but Dunmore is able to rescue a precious point with a precise header.										

LEAGUE DIVISION 1 — Manager: Johnny Carey — SEASON 1962-63

Positions 1–11 listed for each match as **Orient** (top) / *Opponent* (bottom).

No 22 — A ARSENAL — 15/12 · Att 29,075 · Pos 22 · (9) · Pt 12 · F-A 0-2 · H-T 0-1

Scorers, Times, and Referees: Baker 11, 56. Ref: A Holland

Pos	1	2	3	4	5	6	7	8	9	10	11
Orient	Pinner	Charlton	Lewis	Gibbs	Bishop	Lea	Deeley	Gregory	Bolland	Graham	McDonald
Arsenal	*McClelland*	*Magill*	*McCullough*	*Barnwell*	*Neill*	*Sneddon*	*MacLeod*	*Strong*	*Baker*	*Eastham*	*Armstrong*

Pinner blunders with two crosses to gift Baker his goals, but makes several saves to prevent a hammering. It's a very ordinary-looking Gunners side, but mediocre sides can beat the O's with ease at the moment. The attack is still the big problem, unable to relieve the overworked defence.

No 23 — H BIRMINGHAM — 22/12 · Att 11,646 · Pos 22 · (15) · Pt 13 · F-A 2-2 · H-T 2-0

Scorers, Times, and Referees: Musgrove 3, Bolland 24 / Bloomfield 57, 83. Ref: J Parkinson

Pos	1	2	3	4	5	6	7	8	9	10	11
Orient	Pinner	Charlton	Lewis	Lucas	Bishop	Lea	Deeley	Gibbs	Bolland	Graham	Musgrove
Birmingham	*Withers*	*Lynn*	*Green*	*Hennessey*	*Foster*	*Beard*	*Hellawell*	*Bloomfield*	*Harris*	*Leek*	*Auld*

Musgrove has been signed from West Ham for £11,000 and he gives his new side the lead with his first touch. Bolland volleys number two, but Birmingham come back strongly. Green punches the ball clear at the end, but penalty decisions rarely go your way when you're at the bottom.

No 24 — A LEICESTER — 26/12 · Att 17,303 · Pos 22 · (3) · Pt 13 · F-A 1-5 · H-T 0-4

Scorers, Times, and Referees: Musgrove 88 (Ch'brough 21, Ap'ton 40) / Charlton 4 (og), Keyworth 19, 70. Ref: E Jennings

Pos	1	2	3	4	5	6	7	8	9	10	11
Orient	Pinner	Charlton	Lewis	Gibbs	Bishop	Lea	Deeley	Bolland	Dunmore	Graham	Musgrove
Leicester	*Banks*	*Sjoberg*	*Norman*	*McLintock*	*King*	*Appleton*	*Cheesebrough*	*Gibson*	*Keyworth*	*Cross*	*Stringfellow*

Defender Frank McLintock's shot is deflected into the net by Charlton after four minutes, and this sets the tone for the whole game, as the Scottish stopper spends as much time in the Orient half as he does his own. The O's defenders never seem able to stop working for a minute.

No 25 — H FULHAM — 16/2 · Att 17,132 · Pos 22 · (21) · Pt 14 · F-A 1-1 · H-T 0-0

Scorers, Times, and Referees: Graham 55 / Cook 50. Ref: J Loynton

Pos	1	2	3	4	5	6	7	8	9	10	11
Orient	George	Charlton	Lewis	Gibbs	Bishop	Lea	Deeley	Bolland	Dunmore	Graham	Musgrove
Fulham	*Macedo*	*Cohen*	*Langley*	*Mullery*	*Lowe*	*Robson*	*Leggat*	*Cook*	*Brown S*	*Haynes*	*Stratton*

Orient's first League game for 56 days is a critical relegation battle. Johnny Haynes returns from injury, but is matched all the way by Gibbs, who is an effective replacement for the injured Lucas. Deeley creates the equaliser, but embarrassingly misses the 'winner' from three yards.

No 26 — H MANCHESTER C — 23/2 · Att 12,464 · Pos 22 · (18) · Pt 15 · F-A 1-1 · H-T 1-1

Scorers, Times, and Referees: Elwood 14 / Harley 34. Ref: P Bye

Pos	1	2	3	4	5	6	7	8	9	10	11
Orient	George	Charlton	Lewis	Lucas	Bishop	Lea	Deeley	Bolland	Dunmore	Elwood	Musgrove
Manchester C	*Dowd*	*Betts*	*Sear*	*Benson*	*Leivers*	*Oakes*	*Dobing*	*Kennedy*	*Harley*	*Cheetham*	*Hannah*

City are playing a unique 2-5-3 combination, but it doesn't look like a formation that anyone else will want to try. Powder-puff Orient are easily able to outwit the Citizens and deserve to gain a couple of points. A clearance rebounds off the bemused Harley for the equaliser.

No 27 — A BLACKPOOL — 2/3 · Att 11,732 · Pos 22 · (17) · Pt 15 · F-A 2-3 · H-T 0-1

Scorers, Times, and Referees: Dunmore 72, Deeley 81p / Quinn 6p, Charlton 47 (og), McPhee 63. Ref: H Webb

Pos	1	2	3	4	5	6	7	8	9	10	11
Orient	George	Charlton	Lewis	Lucas	Bishop	Lea	Deeley	Gibbs	Dunmore	Bolland	Elwood
Blackpool	*Waiters*	*Armfield*	*Martin*	*Crawford*	*Gratrix*	*Durie*	*Lea*	*Quinn*	*Napier*	*McPhee*	*Horne*

Lea clumsily knocks into a tangerine-clad player to concede the early penalty. The O's cling on, but suffer further when Charlton's foot deflects a shot past George. Orient fight back gamely from 0-3 down, but by then it's far too late. The injured Musgrove is badly missed.

No 28 — H ASTON VILLA — 9/3 · Att 11,509 · Pos 22 · (7) · Pt 15 · F-A 0-2 · H-T 0-2

Scorers, Times, and Referees: Woosnam 6, Wylie 38. Ref: G Hartley

Pos	1	2	3	4	5	6	7	8	9	10	11
Orient	Robertson	Charlton	Lewis	Lucas	Bishop	Lea	Deeley	Gibbs	Dunmore	Bolland	Musgrove
Aston Villa	*Sidebottom*	*Fraser*	*Aitken*	*Tindall*	*Crowe*	*Deakin*	*Ewing*	*Baker*	*Woosnam*	*Wylie*	*Burrows*

Woosnam is used to scoring at Brisbane Road, but unfortunately the ex-Oriental (1955-58) now plays for Villa. A gale-force wind aids Villa in the first half and keeper Sidebottom nearly scores. Even with the help of record-signing Mason, Orient only muster one shot in the second half.

No 29 — H NOTT'M FOREST — 23/3 · Att 14,079 · Pos 22 · (9) · Pt 15 · F-A 0-1 · H-T 0-0

Scorers, Times, and Referees: Addison 54. Ref: J Cattlin

Pos	1	2	3	4	5	6	7	8	9	10	11
Orient	Robertson	Charlton	Lewis	Lucas	Bishop	Lea	Deeley	Gibbs	Dunmore	Bolland	Musgrove
Nott'm Forest	*Grummitt*	*Wilson*	*Mochan*	*Whitefoot*	*McKinlay*	*Winfield*	*Hockey*	*Addison*	*Vowden*	*Quigley*	*Cobb*

Another bad day at the office for the forwards, who cannot penetrate a very average Forest defence. The ice has all gone now, but there is mud in abundance. A Quigley shot hits the post and sticks on the goal-line mud. Charlton clears, but Addison hoofs it back into the net for the goal.

No 30 — A TOTTENHAM — 27/3 · Att 40,260 · Pos 22 · (1) · Pt 15 · F-A 0-2 · H-T 0-1

Scorers, Times, and Referees: Smith 23, Greaves 67p. Ref: E Jennings

Pos	1	2	3	4	5	6	7	8	9	10	11
Orient	Pinner	Charlton	Lewis	Lucas	Bishop	Lea	Deeley	Mason	Dunmore	Graham	Musgrove
Tottenham	*Hollowbread*	*Hopkins*	*Henry*	*Marchi*	*Norman*	*Mackay*	*Saul*	*White*	*Smith*	*Greaves*	*Jones*

Greaves, Saul and Jones are subdued on the muddy pitch, but the difference is the barnstorming Bobby Smith who hits the post twice in earlier attacks before heading the opener. Lea's two-footed tackle from behind on Greaves concedes a penalty and earns him a booking for protesting.

No 31 — A WOLVERHAMPTON — 30/3 · Att 13,739 · Pos 22 · (5) · Pt 15 · F-A 1-2 · H-T 0-2

Scorers, Times, and Referees: Graham 50 / Stobart 2, Wharton 39. Ref: K Hanham

Pos	1	2	3	4	5	6	7	8	9	10	11
Orient	Pinner	Charlton	Lewis	Lucas	Bishop	Gibbs	Deeley	Mason	Dunmore	Graham	Musgrove
Wolverhampton	*Davies*	*Showell*	*Thomson*	*Kirkham*	*Woodfield*	*Flowers*	*Wharton*	*Crowe*	*Stobart*	*Broadbent*	*Hinton*

Deeley (a Wolves favourite for over ten years) receives a hero's welcome. Mason (who walked out after being dropped for the '60 Cup Final) is roundly booed. The five-game goal-drought ends, but the sight of Deeley firing over from three yards is typical of Orient's woeful finishing.

Orient League Matches 32–42

No.	H/A	Opponent	Date	Att.	P			Res	Score	Orient scorer(s)	Opposition scorer(s)	Referee
32	H	LEICESTER	3/4	14,780	22	2	15	L	0-2	—	Stringfellow 7, 36	R Aldous
33	H	BOLTON	12/4	15,369	22	16	15	L	0-1	—	Butler 63p	J Osborne
34	A	IPSWICH	13/4	18,678	22	20	16	D	1-1	Musgrove 42	Moran 63	E Jennings
35	A	BOLTON	15/4	16,649	22	17	18	W	1-0	Dunmore 50	—	K Howley
36	H	BLACKBURN	20/4	8,274	22	14	19	D	1-1	Dunmore 58	Pickering 14	A Sparling
37	A	SHEFFIELD UTD	26/4	20,703	22	7	19	L	0-2	—	Jones 22, Hartle 71	R Faulkner
38	H	LIVERPOOL	2/5	8,273	22	8	21	W	2-1	Graham 16, Bishop 18	St John 44	J Cooke
39	A	SHEFFIELD WED	4/5	20,762	22	6	21	L	1-3	Graham 27	Dobson 21, Finney 59, Fantham 74	H Hough
40	H	BURNLEY	7/5	10,085	22	4	21	L	0-1	—	Towers 20	R Smith
41	A	WEST HAM	11/5	16,746	22	13	21	L	0-2	—	Brabrook 17, Scott 84	G McCabe
42	A	MANCHESTER U	18/5	32,759	22	18	21	L	1-3	Dunmore 9	Charlton 80 (og), Law 81, Charlton 85	H Horner

Home Average 16,489 — Away Average 23,797

Line-ups and match reports

32 – v Leicester
Orient: Pinner, Charlton, Lewis, Lucas, Bishop, Gibbs, Deeley, Mason, Dunmore, Graham, Musgrove.
Leicester: Banks, Chalmers, Norman, McClintock, King, Appleton, Riley, Cross, Keyworth, Heath, Stringfellow.
Leicester, not content with ending Orient's FA Cup dreams, also look like ensuring their league survival hopes are equally forlorn. This time, there's little fight from the O's and the Foxes are able to grab the points whilst on cruise control, thanks to Mike Stringfellow's two headers.

33 – v Bolton
Orient: Pinner, Charlton, Lewis, Lucas, Bishop, Lea, Gregory, Mason, Dunmore, Graham, Elwood.
Bolton: Hopkinson, Hartle, Farrimond, Rimmer, Edwards, Lennard, Birch, Russell, Davies, Hill, Butler.
Bolton's keeper Hopkinson limps off for 18 minutes after a collision with his own centre-half, but Orient find his temporary replacement Farrimond is capable of making two fine saves. Lewis concedes the penalty after a weak short pass is cut out by Davies who is duly upended.

34 – v Ipswich
Orient: Pinner, Charlton, Taylor, Lucas, Bishop, Lea, Mason, Dunmore, Musgrove, Bolland, Elwood.
Ipswich: Bailey, Carberry, Compton, Baxter, Nelson, Elsworthy, Stephenson, Moran, Crawford, Phillips, Leadbetter.
Ipswich look as though they might become the first League champions to be relegated the following season. They are as bad as Orient, which makes for a deadly-dull game. Musgrove gives Orient the novelty of a lead, but Moran levels when he pounces on a rebound off the goalpost.

35 – v Bolton
Orient: Pinner, Charlton, Taylor, Lucas, Bishop, Lea, Mason, Dunmore, Musgrove, Graham, Elwood.
Bolton: Smith, Hartle, Hatton, Rimmer, Edwards, Lennard, Russell, Davies, Davies, Hill, Birch.
Orient's longest-ever sequence of winless League games (23) finally comes to an end after nearly seven months. The O's defence gamely stops Bolton's attacks, paving the way for the victory. Dunmore's shot gets a slight deflection, but nobody could say Orient don't deserve some luck.

36 – v Blackburn
Orient: Pinner, Charlton, Taylor, Lucas, Bishop, Lea, Mason, Dunmore, Musgrove, Deeley, Elwood.
Blackburn: Else, Bray, Taylor, McGrath, Woods, Newton, Douglas, McEvoy, Pickering, Ferguson, Harrison.
The casual fans have now deserted Brisbane Road leaving just the hardcore rump of fans. It's a pity because Orient have now started to pick up points, albeit too late to save themselves from the inevitable drop. The O's are now using more long balls as short ones are sticking in the mud.

37 – v Sheffield Utd
Orient: Pinner, Charlton, Taylor, Lucas, Bishop, Lea, Mason, Dunmore, Musgrove, Deeley, Elwood.
Sheffield Utd: Hodgkinson, Badger, Shaw B, Richardson, Shaw J, Summers, Allchurch, Wagstaff, Pace, Jones, Hartle.
Blades boss John Harris correctly judges he can use four teenagers in his experimental line-up and still beat the hapless O's. Mick Jones scores with a trademark header that Leeds fans from the 70's would recognise, whilst Len Badger plays the first of his 458 league games for the U's.

38 – v Liverpool
Orient: Pinner, Charlton, Taylor, Lucas, Bishop, Lea, Mason, Dunmore, Musgrove, Graham, Elwood.
Liverpool: Lawrence, Byrne, Thomson, Milne, Lawler, Stevenson, Callaghan, Hunt, St John, Wallace, A'Court.
One more O's fan has deserted since the last home game, but he or she misses the first victory here in the League for 14 games (eight months). Orient stun Pool with two goals in 90 seconds to effectively win the game. The O's fans invade the pitch at the end to celebrate victory wildly.

39 – v Sheffield Wed
Orient: Pinner, Charlton, Taylor, Lucas, Bishop, Lea, Bolland, Deeley, Musgrove, Graham, Elwood.
Sheffield Wed: Springett, Johnson, Megson, McAnearney, Swan, Young, Finney, Quinn, Layne, Fantham, Dobson.
Bolland replaces the injured Mason in the line-up, but the best O's players are Pinner, who denies his old club several would-be goals, and Bishop, who nullifies the threat of Bronco Layne. Alas, Finney and Fantham are free to score the goals that confirm that Orient are relegated.

40 – v Burnley
Orient: George, Charlton, Taylor, Lucas, Bishop, Lea, Elwood, Dunmore, Musgrove, Bolland, Graham.
Burnley: Blacklaw, Angus, Elder, Adamson, Talbot, Miller, Meredith, Lochhead, Bellamy, Towers, Harris.
Orient's last-ever top-flight home game is a noisy encounter as 10,000 O's fans roar their team on. Their efforts go unrewarded as George is a bit slow to get to Harry Towers's shot. Elwood has a golden opportunity to level two minutes from time, but sends his effort wide of the post.

41 – v West Ham
Orient: Pinner, Charlton, Taylor, Lucas, Bishop, Lea, Mason, Dunmore, Musgrove, Bolland, Elwood.
West Ham: Leslie, Bond, Burkett, Peters, Brown, Moore, Brabrook, Boyce, Byrne, Sealey, Scott.
Ex-Hammer Musgrove is made captain for the day to try to inspire those around him, but the Hammers are still able to sleepwalk to victory. Relegation is now confirmed, but the faithful O's fans sing 'Dear Old Pals' and 'The O's Go Marching On' with typical East London gusto.

42 – v Manchester U
Orient: George, Charlton, Taylor, Lucas, Bishop, Lea, Mason, Dunmore, Musgrove, Bolland, Elwood.
Manchester U: Gaskell, Dunne, Cantwell, Crerand, Foulkes, Setters, Quixall, Herd, Law, Giles, Charlton.
The Red Devils can't afford to think about next week's Cup final appearance, because they still could go down. Bobby Charlton's shot is deflected in by Stan Charlton. Law's genius soon makes it two before Bobby strikes again. Two legends sign off O's top-flight career in style.

LEAGUE DIVISION 1 (CUP-TIES) Manager: Johnny Carey SEASON 1962-63

League Cup

Pos	1	2	3	4	5	6	7	8	9	10	11

2 A NEWCASTLE — 17 D — 22,490 2:5 — F-A 1-1 — H-T 0-0 — 26/9
Scorers/Times/Referees: Bolland 49 | Fell 86p | Ref: J Thacker

	1	2	3	4	5	6	7	8	9	10	11
Orient	George	Charlton	Taylor	Lucas	Clark	Lea	Deeley	Bolland	Dunmore	Waites	McDonald
Newcastle	Hollins	Keith	McMichael	Neale	McGrath	Iley	Day	Hilley	Thomas	Hale	Fell

Bolland heads in Deeley's corner to light up a poor game, but Deeley has a goal ruled out soon afterwards. George is injured after 73 minutes and Charlton is the emergency keeper. Newcastle's blushes are spared when Lucas illegally punches away a header to concede the penalty.

2R H NEWCASTLE — 12 W — 8,037 2:2 — F-A 4-2 aet — H-T 2-1 — 1/10
Scorers/Times/Referees: Boll'd 11, Graham 25, 114, Deeley 116 | Lucas 5 (og), Suddick 85 | Ref: R Aldous

	1	2	3	4	5	6	7	8	9	10	11
Orient	Robertson	Charlton	Lewis	Lucas	Clark	Lea	Deeley	Bolland	Dunmore	Graham	McDonald
Newcastle	Hollins	Keith	McGrath	Neale	Thompson	Dalton	Hilley	Suddick	Thomas	Kerray	Fell

Alan Suddick does all he can for the Magpies, crossing for the opening (own) goal and sending the tie into extra-time, but it's Dunmore who Geordie legend Jackie Milburn implies is the finest centre-forward in England. The floodlights fail for seven minutes, early in extra-time.

3 H CHESTER — 19 W — 7,428 4:21 — F-A 9-2 — H-T 3-0 — 17/10
Scorers/Times/Referees: Waites 9, 65, 80, Dun' 38,49, Deel' 44, Greg' 81, Myers' 86 [Gra' 46, 52, 85] | Ref: J Cooke

	1	2	3	4	5	6	7	8	9	10	11
Orient	Robertson	Charlton	Taylor	Gibbs	Bishop	Lea	Deeley	Waites	Dunmore	Graham	Wedge
Chester	Hardie	Molyneux	Fleming	Wilson	Butler	Corbishley	Gregson	Myerscough	Fitzgerald	Clarke	Jones

Orient's front line queue up to wreak spectacular damage to Chester's pride. Waites and Graham get hat-tricks, and the only member of the forward line not to score is Roger Wedge in his only Orient appearance. They last won a game 9-2 against Aldershot in 1934 in Division 3 (S).

4 H CHARLTON — 22 W — 9,602 2:17 — F-A 3-2 — H-T 3-2 — 12/11
Scorers/Times/Referees: Foster 18, 33 Gregory 28 | Matthews 5, Peacock 34 | Ref: T Davies

	1	2	3	4	5	6	7	8	9	10	11
Orient	George	Charlton	Taylor	Lucas	Bishop	Gibbs	Deeley	Gregory	Dunmore	Foster	McDonald
Charlton	Wakeham	Sewell	Hewie	Tocknell	Hinton	Bailey	Kennedy	Matthews	Matthews	Peacock	Kinsey

A crackling cup-tie that sees five goals in the first half as both sides go for all-out attack. Debutant Harry Gregory gets in on the act when he races through and blasts in the goal which gives Orient the lead. After the interval, Orient shut up shop and soak up all the non-stop pressure.

5 H BURY — 22 L — 6,094 2:2 — F-A 0-2 — H-T 0-1 — 3/12
Scorers/Times/Referees: Calder 7, Jones 81 | Ref: D Smith

	1	2	3	4	5	6	7	8	9	10	11
Orient	Pinner	Charlton	Lewis	Gibbs	Bishop	Lea	Deeley	Gregory	Dunmore	Taylor	McDonald
Bury	Harker	Robertson	Eastham	Turner	Stokoe	Atherton	Mayers	Jones	Calder	Beaumont	Bartley

The fog descends on Brisbane Road, but it isn't thick enough to warrant abandonment, nor to shroud the horrors of this performance from the home fans. Calder takes advantage of a sloppy defence and then sets 18-year-old Jones on his successful run through Orient's tired defence.

FA Cup

3 H HULL — 22 D — 9,757 3:15 — F-A 1-1 — H-T 0-1 — 11/2
Scorers/Times/Referees: Musgrove 55 | Chilton 38 | Ref: K Stokes

	1	2	3	4	5	6	7	8	9	10	11
Orient	George	Charlton	Lewis	Gibbs	Bishop	Lea	Deeley	Bolland	Dunmore	Graham	Musgrove
Hull	Williams	Davidson	Sharpe	Collinson	Garvey	McMillan	Clarke	Henderson	Chilton	Cummins	McSeveney

After nine postponements in five weeks the match finally takes place on a still-frozen pitch. Chilton nips in to convert a rebound, but Musgrove continues his 100% scoring record with a 25-yard blockbuster. Neither side must relish a replay with such a backlog of matches awaiting them.

3R A HULL — 22 W — 14,214 3:15 — F-A 2-0 aet — H-T 0-0 — 19/2
Scorers/Times/Referees: Musgrove 95, Gibbs 115 | Ref: K Stokes

	1	2	3	4	5	6	7	8	9	10	11
Orient	George	Charlton	Lewis	Gibbs	Bishop	Lea	Deeley	Bolland	Dunmore	Graham	Musgrove
Hull	Williams	Davidson	Sharpe	Collinson	Garvey	McMillan	Clarke	Henderson	Chilton	Cummins	McSeveney

With the prospect of thirty minutes of extra-time, O's skipper Charlton pleads for an abandonment as the Boothferry Road pitch is ploughed up into a muddy and snowy gloop. Hull's captain Davidson persuades the ref to carry on, then instantly regrets it as Musgrove strikes again.

4 H DERBY — 22 W — 12,607 2:19 — F-A 3-0 — H-T 1-0 — 4/3
Scorers/Times/Referees: Dunmore 7, Elwood 70, Deeley 90 | Ref: F Cowen

	1	2	3	4	5	6	7	8	9	10	11
Orient	Robertson	Charlton	Lewis	Lucas	Bishop	Lea	Deeley	Gibbs	Dunmore	Bolland	Elwood
Derby	Oxford	Barrowcliffe	Ferguson	Young	Moors	Waller	Stephenson	Parry	Curry	Hutchinson	McCann

O's keeper George is injured and Pinner is cup-tied, so 37-year-old Robertson is recalled. He first signed for Chelsea in 1946. Orient might not be good enough for the First Division, but they are still far superior to most Second Division sides. A pity they've drawn Leicester City then.

5 H LEICESTER — 22 L — 25,769 2 — F-A 0-1 — H-T 0-1 — 16/3
Scorers/Times/Referees: Keyworth 6 | Ref: T Dawes

	1	2	3	4	5	6	7	8	9	10	11
Orient	Robertson	Charlton	Lewis	Lucas	Bishop	Lea	Deeley	Bolland	Dunmore	Elwood	Musgrove
Leicester	Banks	Sjoberg	Norman	McLintock	King	Appleton	Riley	Cross	Keyworth	Gibson	Stringfellow

For the third consecutive Saturday, Orient succumb to a goal after six minutes. For the rest of the match they swarm forward like enraged killer bees, but unfortunately they come across the legendary Gordon Banks who is prepared to get himself knocked out to preserve his clean sheet.

	P	W	D	L	F	A	W	D	L	F	A	Pts
		Home					**Away**					
1 Everton	42	14	7	0	48	17	11	4	6	36	25	61
2 Tottenham	42	14	6	1	72	28	9	3	9	39	34	55
3 Burnley	42	14	4	3	41	17	8	6	7	37	40	54
4 Leicester	42	14	6	1	53	23	6	6	9	26	30	52
5 Wolves	42	11	6	4	51	25	9	4	8	42	40	50
6 Sheffield Wed	42	10	5	6	38	26	9	5	7	39	37	48
7 Arsenal	42	11	4	6	44	33	7	6	8	42	44	46
8 Liverpool	42	13	3	5	45	22	4	7	10	26	37	44
9 Nottingham F	42	12	4	5	39	28	5	6	10	28	41	44
10 Sheffield Utd	42	11	7	3	33	20	5	5	11	25	40	44
11 Blackburn R	42	11	4	6	55	34	4	8	9	24	37	42
12 West Ham	42	8	6	7	39	34	6	6	9	34	35	40
13 Blackpool	42	8	7	6	34	27	5	7	9	24	37	40
14 West Brom	42	11	1	9	40	37	5	6	10	31	42	39
15 Aston Villa	42	12	2	7	38	23	3	3	12	24	45	38
16 Fulham	42	8	6	7	28	30	6	4	11	22	41	38
17 Ipswich	42	5	8	8	34	39	7	3	11	25	39	35
18 Bolton	42	13	3	5	35	18	2	2	17	20	57	35
19 Manchester U	42	6	6	9	36	38	6	4	11	31	43	34
20 Birmingham	42	6	8	7	40	40	4	5	12	23	50	33
21 Manchester C	42	7	5	9	30	45	3	6	12	28	57	31
22 LEYTON O	42	4	5	12	22	37	2	4	15	15	44	21
	924	223	113	126	895	641	126	113	223	641	895	924

Odds & ends

Double wins: (0).

Double losses: (9) Arsenal, Aston Villa, Blackpool, Burnley, Leicester, Sheffield W, Tottenham, West Brom, Wolves.

Won from behind: (0).

Lost from in front: (2) Ipswich (h), Manchester U (a).

High spots: Beating the eventual champions Everton 3-0.
McDonald's wonder goal that defeated Manchester U.
Reaching the fifth round of both cup competitions.
Beating Chester 9-2 in the League Cup.

Low spots: Losing First Division status so tamely.
Only scoring 37 goals in 42 League games.
Going over six months without a League win.
Only filling up Brisbane Road for one League game (Spurs).

Ever-presents: (1) Charlton.
Hat-tricks: (2) Waites, Graham (League Cup).
Leading scorer: Dunmore, Graham (14).

	Appearances			Goals			
	Lge	LC	FAC	Lge	LC	FAC	Tot
Bishop, Sid	39	3	4		1		1
Bolland, Gordon	24	2	4	3	2		5
Charlton, Stan	42	5	4				
Clark, Dave	3	2					
Deeley, Norman	36	5	4	5	2	1	8
Dunmore, David	37	5	4	11	2	1	14
Elwood, Joe	11		2	1		1	2
Foster, George	4	1			2		2
George, Frank	7	2	2				
Gibbs, Derek	17	3	3	1		1	2
Graham, Malcolm	27	2	2	9	5		14
Gregory, Harry	6	2		1	1		2
Lea, Cyril	40	4	4				
Lewis, Eddie	28	2	4				
Lucas, Malcolm	37	3	2				
McDonald, Terry	20	4		2			2
Mason, Bob	13						
Musgrove, Malcolm	18		3	3	2		5
Pinner, Michael	19	1					
Robertson, Willie	16	2	2				
Taylor, Willie	16	4					
Waites, George	2	2			3		3
Wedge, R	2	1					
23 players used	462	55	44	37	17	6	60

LEYTON ORIENT—Standing: Lucas, Lea, Bishop, Robertson, Graham, Lewis. Sitting—
Deeley, Dunmore, Charlton, Gibbs, McDonald.

Their names will forever be immortalised among supporters of Leyton Orient FC.
The players who gave the O's their Season in the Sun